After Faed.

WILLIAM SHAKESPEARE.

SHAKESPEARE'S

COMEDY OF

THE MERCHANT OF VENICE

EDITED, WITH NOTES

BY

WILLIAM J. ROLFE, Litt.D.

FORMERLY HEAD MASTER OF THE HIGH SCHOOL
CAMBRIDGE, MASS.

ILLUSTRATED

NEW YORK ·:· CINCINNATI ·:· CHICAGO
AMERICAN BOOK COMPANY

PREFACE

My edition of *The Merchant of Venice* was first published in 1870. It was the initial volume of the complete edition of Shakespeare's plays and poems, in forty
volumes, which was finished in 1883.

As I stated in the original preface, the book was
planned and nearly completed more than three years
earlier, but was laid aside for other work and not taken
up again until the summer of 1870. Meanwhile the
notes had been used with classes in school and out of
school, and received such revision as was suggested by
that experience and by further study of Shakespeare.

When I began to prepare the book, Shakespeare was
just coming to be studied in the secondary schools.
Only a few annotated editions of single plays had been
published in England, and none, so far as I am aware,
in this country. Helps for the school study of Shakespeare were few and expensive. The Cowden-Clarke
Concordance cost ten or twelve dollars. The first volume of Dr. Furness's "New Variorum" edition (*Romeo
and Juliet*) was published in 1871, but the second (*Mac-
beth*, the first of the plays commonly read in schools)
not until 1873. Critical commentaries on Shakespeare
were, as a rule, to be had only in costly English editions. High school libraries were few and small, and
public libraries, except in the larger cities, contained
but little Shakespearian literature. Few teachers in
secondary schools throughout the country were better
equipped than I was, some fifteen years earlier, when

the only *Shakespeare* I had was a one-volume edition without notes, and my pupils had to use such editions as they found at home or among their friends.

In editing this play, therefore, it was my aim, as I said in the preface, to furnish " a pure *text* and the *notes* needed for its thorough elucidation and illustration." Having in mind the needs of the teacher as well as the student, I preferred, in these notes, to err, if at all, on the side of fullness. The book was favourably received, but the publishers were surprised, as I was, when the demand for similar editions of all the plays generally read in schools and colleges was followed by a call from the reading public for the rest of Shakespeare's works in the same form.

The changes made now in revising the book have been mainly due to the changes that have taken place in the educational situation during the past thirty-five years. For instance, I have omitted the greater part of the notes on *textual variations*. This play, with most of the others read in schools, is now among the twelve plays that Dr. Furness has edited. No teacher can afford to do without his encyclopedic volumes, in which all the readings and notes of the early editions and of the standard modern editions are epitomized, together with large extracts from the best commentaries and much admirable criticism by Dr. Furness himself. The textual readings, however, are for the average teacher the least important part of the material in that monumental edition. The text of Shakespeare is now virtually settled. Many emendations have been proposed in recent years, but those that have been generally accepted could be counted on the fingers of one hand, with possibly a finger or two to spare. Scattered *cruces*, due to the corruption of the earlier editions, still remain to perplex the critics, who will probably quarrel over them to the end of time ; and to some of these, as illustrations of an interesting but exasperating class of Shakespearian problems, I make brief reference in the present notes.

I have also omitted most of the " Critical Comments " from the introduction, as the books from which they were taken are now readily accessible in public and school libraries. For these extracts I have substituted familiar comments of my own, and have added more of the same kind in the Appendix. A concise account of Shakespeare's *metre* has also been inserted as an introduction to the notes.

Minor changes have been made throughout the notes. Some have been abridged or condensed, some have been expanded, and new ones have been added here and there. In very few instances, however, have I found it necessary to make any radical alterations, as the work of revision has been going on ever since the book was published. It has been so often reprinted that I have had opportunities every year — sometimes several times in a year — for making the slight changes and additions that seemed to be necessary or desirable. In 1883, when line numbers were first inserted, new plates were required, and the introduction and notes were thoroughly revised. More than five pages were added to the introduction, and about five more were afterwards appended to the notes.

The present edition is, nevertheless, substantially a new book, and many teachers will, I think, prefer it to the old one. Both can be used, without serious inconvenience, in the same class or club.

I may add that, in the revision, I have not been inclined to insert the " Hints for Teachers " that are to be found in some good school editions. The teacher who does not need them must regard them as an impertinence. Those who do need them are, in my opinion, quite as likely to misuse them as to profit by them. If they are made full enough and explicit enough to be of real service to the young and inexperienced teacher, they should be printed in a separate booklet, like my *Elementary Study of English*, which was prepared mainly as a guide to the use of certain books for younger students. I intend to prepare something of the kind on the study of Shakespeare.

CONTENTS

MONUMENT AT STRATFORD

JOHN SHAKESPEARE'S HOUSE IN HENLEY STREET

THE LIFE AND WORKS OF SHAKESPEARE

His Life. — William Shakespeare was born at Stratford-upon-Avon, in the county of Warwick, England, in April, 1564. He was baptized on the 26th of April (Old Style) ; and, as it was a common practice to christen infants when three days old, the tradition which makes his birthday the 23d (May 3, as dates are now reckoned) is generally accepted. His father, John Shakespeare, who had been a farmer in a neighbouring village, came to Stratford about 1553, and adopted the trade of a glover. His mother, Mary Arden, belonged to a younger branch of a good old Warwickshire family, and inherited a considerable estate from her father. John Shakespeare was evidently shrewd, energetic, ambitious, and public-spirited. He made money, and was popular with his fellow-townsmen.   After passing through the lower grades of office, he was elected alderman, and in 1568 became high bailiff or mayor.

INNER COURT OF THE GRAMMAR SCHOOL, STRATFORD

Of a family of four sons and four daughters, William was the third child, but the eldest son.   When he was seven years old, he was doubtless sent to the Stratford grammar school, where he got all the regular schooling he ever had.   In 1582, when he was only eighteen, he married Anne Hathaway, of the hamlet of Shottery, near

Stratford, who was some eight years older than himself. A daughter was born to him in 1583, and twins — a boy and a girl — two years later. He had no other children.

It was probably in the next year, 1586, that Shakespeare went to London, where he became, first an actor, then a writer for the stage. As an actor he seems to have made no special mark, but as a writer he very soon distinguished himself, and in a few years had won the foremost rank among the dramatists of his time. In 1598, Francis Meres, in his *Palladis Tamia, or Wit's*

Treasury, speaks of him as " the most excellent among the English for both kinds of tragedy and comedy." His works not only became widely popular, but they brought him special marks of favour and approval from Queen Elizabeth and her successor, James, and gained

CHAPEL OF GUILD AND GRAMMAR SCHOOL

for him the patronage and friendship of some of the most accomplished men of rank of that day.

But while thus prosperous and honoured in London, Shakespeare continued to look upon Stratford as his home. There he had left his wife and children, and thither, after he had secured a competency, he returned to spend the evening of his days. It was probably about the year 1611 that he settled down in Stratford, at New Place, an estate purchased in 1597. His wife was still living, and also his two daughters, of whom the elder, Susanna, was married in June, 1607, to Dr. John Hall, an eminent physician of the time. The younger daughter, Judith, was married to Mr. Thomas Quiney, a Stratford vintner, in February, 1616. Hamnet, the poet's son, had died in 1596, in his twelfth year.

Shakespeare died at Stratford on the 23d of April, 1616, and was buried in the parish church.

The poet's family became extinct with his grandchildren. Elizabeth, the only child of the Halls, was twice married, but had no offspring. Thomas and Judith Quiney had three sons, one of whom died in babyhood, the others at eighteen and twenty respectively. Judith lived to the age of seventy-six, dying in February, 1638. Lady Barnard (Elizabeth Hall) died in February, 1669, at the age of sixty-one.

His Works. — The first work of Shakespeare which was printed with his name was the poem of *Venus and Adonis*, which appeared in 1593. In the dedication to the Earl of Southampton the author styles it "the first heir of his invention." In 1594, *The Rape of Lucrece* was published. Both these poems were reprinted several times in the poet's lifetime. His only other works, besides the plays, are a few of the pieces in *The Passionate Pilgrim* (a small collection of poems, first printed in 1599), and his *Sonnets* (154 in number), with a poem entitled *A Lover's Complaint*, which appeared together in 1609.

The first edition of his collected dramatic works contained all the plays generally included in modern editions, with the exception of *Pericles*, and was published in a folio volume, in 1623, or not till seven years after his death.   It was put forth by two of his friends

FIRESIDE. — KITCHEN OF HOUSE IN HENLEY STREET

and fellow-actors, *John Heminge* and *Henrie Condell*, and the title-page declares it to be printed "according to the true original copies."   The preface also condemns all preceding editions of separate plays[1] as

---

[1] Eighteen of the plays are known to have been separately printed, some of them more than once, in Shakespeare's lifetime.   *Othello* was also printed separately in 1622.   All these editions are in quarto form, and are commonly known as the old or early *quartos*.

" stolen and surreptitious copies, maimed and deformed by the frauds and stealths of injurious impostors," while it claims that the publishers of this volume had the use of the author's manuscripts. They probably had the use of such of his papers as were in the possession of the Blackfriars Theatre, to which they, like himself, belonged. The volume, however, had no proper editing, and every page is disfigured by the grossest typographical errors. While it is the earliest and the only authentic edition of the plays, it cannot be accepted as anything like an infallible authority in all cases for what Shakespeare actually wrote. The quartos, though they were all piratical ventures, are of considerable value in the correction of its errors and imperfections.

The volume just described is commonly known as the " first folio." A second folio edition, including the same plays, appeared in 1632. It contains some new readings, which are probably nothing more than the conjectural emendations of the unknown editor.

The third folio, a reprint of the second, with few variations of any value or interest, was first published in 1663. It was reissued the next year, with the addition of seven plays: *Pericles*, *The London Prodigal*, *Thomas Lord Cromwell*, *Sir John Oldcastle*, *The Puritan Widow*, *A Yorkshire Tragedy*, and *Locrine*. *Pericles* is the only one of these in which Shakespeare could have had any hand.

A fourth and last folio was brought out in 1685. It was a reprint of that of 1664 (including the seven plays just mentioned), with the spelling somewhat modernized, but few other changes.

These four folios were the only editions of the plays brought out in the seventeenth century. The eighteenth century produced a long succession of editors — Rowe, Pope, Theobald, Hanmer, Warburton, Johnson, Steevens, Capell, Reed, Malone, and Rann. In 1803 (2d edition, 1813) appeared what is known as *Reed's Second Edition of Johnson and Steevens*, in twenty-one volumes, in which were incorporated most of the notes of the preceding editions. This was followed by the *Variorum of 1821*, also in twenty-one volumes, mostly prepared by Malone, but completed and carried through the press by his friend Boswell. The most important English editions of more recent date are those of Knight, Collier, Singer, Staunton, Dyce, Clark and Wright (the "Cambridge" edition), Charles and Mary Cowden-Clarke, Halliwell-Phillipps, and Irving and Marshall (the "Henry Irving" edition). Of American editions the most noteworthy are Verplanck's (1847), Hudson's (1855 and 1881), Grant White's (1857–1865 and 1883), and Furness's ("New Variorum" edition; begun in 1871).

COLONNADE OF DUCAL PALACE, VENICE

INTRODUCTION TO THE MERCHANT OF VENICE

The History of the Play

The Merchant of Venice is the last on a list of Shakespeare's plays given by Francis Meres in his *Palladis Tamia*, 1598. In the same year it was entered as follows on the Register of the Stationers' Company: —

"22 Julii, 1598 James Robertes.] A booke of the Marchaunt of Venyce, or otherwise called the Jewe of

Venyce.   Provided that yt bee not prynted by the said James Robertes, or anye other whatsoever, without lycence first had from the Right honorable the lord Chamberlen."

The company of players to which Shakespeare belonged, and for which he wrote, was " the Lord Chamberlain's Servants "; and the above order was meant to prohibit the publication of the play until the patron of the company should give his permission.   This he appears not to have done until two years later, when the following entry was made in the Register : —

" 28 Octobris, 1600, Thomas haies.] . . . the booke of the merchant of Venyce."

Soon after this entry, or before the end of 1600, the play was published by Heyes in quarto form ; and another edition, also in quarto, was issued the same year by Roberts.

Philip Henslowe, a theatrical manager of the time, in his *Diary*, in which he kept his accounts, with the dates of plays that he brought out, etc. (a book of great value to students of dramatic history), records, under the date " 25 of aguste, 1594," the performance of " the Venesyon comodey," which is marked *ne*, as a new play.   Some critics take this to be *The Merchant of Venice*, since the company of players to which Shakespeare belonged was then acting at Henslowe's theatre ; but it is quite impossible that the play could have been written as early as 1594.   The more probable date is 1596 or 1597.

THE SOURCES OF THE PLOT

In the plot of *The Merchant of Venice* two distinct stories — that of the bond and that of the caskets — are skilfully interwoven. Both are found in the *Gesta Romanorum*, a Latin collection of fictitious narratives, which had been translated into English as early as the time of Henry VI. It is probable, however, that Shakespeare was indebted, directly or indirectly, for the incidents connected with the bond to a story in *Il Pecorone*, a collection of tales by Giovanni Fiorentino, first published at Milan in 1558, though written almost two centuries earlier. In this story we have a rich lady *at Belmont*, who is to be won on certain conditions of a nature unsuited for dramatic purposes; and she is finally won by a young merchant, whose friend, having become surety for him to a Jew under the same penalty as in the play, is rescued by the adroitness of the married lady, disguised as a lawyer. She receives, as in the play, her marriage ring as a gratuity, and afterwards banters her husband, as Portia does, upon the loss of it. An English translation of the book was extant in Shakespeare's time.

Possibly the dramatist was somewhat indebted to *The Orator*, translated from the French of Alexander Silvayn (London, 1596). Portions of the 95th Declamation in this book are strikingly like some of Shylock's speeches at the trial. It is doubtful whether the old ballad of *Gernutus*, which some critics believe that

Shakespeare used, is earlier or later than the play; but even if it was earlier, it is improbable that he was indebted to it, or to sundry other versions of the story, in prose or verse, which editors and commentators have discovered.

There is good reason, however, to believe that the bond and casket legends had been blended in dramatic form before Shakespeare began to write for the stage. Stephen Gosson, a Puritan author, in his *Schoole of Abuse* (1579), excepts a few plays from the sweeping condemnation of his "plesaunt invective against Poets, Pipers, Plaiers, Jesters, and such-like caterpillers of a Commonwelth." Among these exceptions he mentions "*The Jew*, . . . representing *the greedinesse of worldly chusers*, and *the bloody minds of usurers*." We have no other knowledge of this play of *The Jew;* but the nationality of its hero and the double moral, agreeing so exactly with that of *The Merchant of Venice,* render it probable that the plots of the two dramas were essentially the same, and that Shakespeare, in this instance as in others, worked upon some rough model already prepared for him. The question, however, is not of great importance. "Be the merit of the fable whose it may, the characters, the language, the poetry, and the sentiment are his, and his alone. To no other writer of the period could we be indebted for the charming combination of womanly grace, and dignity, and playfulness which is found in Portia; for the exquisite picture of friendship between Bassanio and Antonio; for the profusion of poetic beauties scattered over the play; and for the masterly delineation of that perfect type of Judaism in olden times, the character of Shylock himself " (Staunton).

Similarly, Mr. Grant White, after referring to Shakespeare's indebtedness for the materials of his plot to the old story-tellers, and probably for their combination in dramatic form to an earlier playwright, asks: " What then remains to Shakespeare? and what is there to show that he is not a plagiarist? Everything that makes *The Merchant of Venice* what it is. The people are puppets, and the incidents are all in these old stories. They are mere bundles of barren sticks that the poet's touch causes to bloom like Aaron's rod; they are heaps of dry bones till he clothes them with human flesh and breathes into them the breath of life. *Antonio*, grave, pensive, prudent save in his devotion to his young kinsman, as a Christian hating the Jew, as a royal merchant despising the usurer; *Bassanio*, lavish yet provident, a generous gentleman although a fortune-seeker, wise although a gay gallant, and manly though dependent; *Gratiano*, who unites the not too common virtues of thorough good nature and unselfishness with the sometimes not unserviceable fault of talking for talk's sake; *Shylock*, crafty and cruel, whose revenge is as mean as it is fierce and furious, whose abuse never rises to invective, and who has yet some dignity of port as the avenger of a nation's wrongs, some claim upon our sympathy as a father outraged by his only child; and

Portia, matchless impersonation of that rare woman who is gifted even more in intellect than loveliness,— these, not to notice minor characters no less perfectly organized or completely developed after their kind — these, and the poetry which is their atmosphere, and through which they beam upon us, all radiant in its golden light, are Shakespeare's only; and these it is, and not the incidents of old and, but for these, forgotten tales, that make *The Merchant of Venice* a priceless and imperishable dower to the queenly city that sits enthroned upon the sea — a dower of romance more bewitching than that of her moonlit waters and beauty-laden balconies, of adornment more splendid than that of her pictured palaces, of human interest more enduring than that of her blood-stained annals, more touching even than the sight of her faded grandeur."

SHAKESPEARE AND ITALY

In *As You Like It*, Rosalind, bantering the affected Jaques on having been in foreign lands and come home only to " disable all the benefits of his own country and be out of love with his nativity," says, " Look you lisp and wear strange suits, or I will scarce think you have swam in a gondola." To have swam in a gondola was to Rosalind — and to Shakespeare, we may say — the typical achievement of a traveller; and it may still be so regarded. There is nothing else so novel in all one's tourist experiences — nothing that so makes one feel his distance from his native land and all its ways and habits.

If he comes by rail to Venice he finds the station much like that in any other large city. He leaves the train, goes with the crowd toward the door, steps out into the open air — and into a new world, or rather an old one, though new to him. It is a step from the nineteenth century to the fifteenth. It seems for the moment like magic. He looks back to see if the railway station has not vanished into thin air; and this seems actually to have happened, for the handsome front of the building might belong to any other structure as well. He is in a small square on the bank of the Grand Canal, where a whole fleet of gondolas is drawn up, waiting for passengers like the hackney carriages at one of our railway terminals. He jumps on board one of them, gives the name of his hotel to the gondolier, and is soon afloat on the marine Broadway of Venice.

It is now that, swimming in a gondola, he really feels the significance of Rosalind's allusion to it. And he is not only in a strange land, but in a long-past age. From the railway train to the gondola is from our land to Venice, and from our day to Shakespeare's. There is something in the noiseless, gliding motion of the craft, especially in this sudden transition to it from the clatter and jar and rush of the train, which adds indescribably to the dreamy, delusive effect. Everything around him is in keeping with the bewildering enchantment. Nothing distinctively modern is to be seen on either hand. He has actually been transported to an old world of history, poetry, and romance, of which hitherto he has had only a vague idea. Soon the gondola turns out of the Grand Canal into one of the narrow canals that afford a short cut across its immense curves, and he is in a stream only a few yards wide, hemmed in by lofty time-worn walls — one of the watery back alleys of the old city; but he emerges upon the Grand Canal again near the Rialto Bridge. The gondolier points it out, but it was not necessary; he could not possibly mistake it. Near the end of the canal he reaches his hotel, fronting upon it. It is an old palace — three or four hundred years old — but for the most part so remodeled within that one could not distinguish it from any modern hotel; and our tourist is back into the twentieth century again as the elevator takes him to his room.

This may seem a long introduction, and rather intended to air my memories of travel, in the manner of our friend Jaques, than to lead up to my subject. I have dwelt upon it as illustrating our entrance upon the study of Shakespeare. In coming to Venice, I have said, we enter upon an old world of history, poetry, and romance; and to such a world of poetry and romance and history does Shakespeare introduce us — a world full of life and action, crowded with personages real and unreal, yet the latter none the less real because they were born of the poet's brain — a world with its England and France, its Greece and Italy, its London, Paris, Rome, and Venice, where we may travel at will without stirring from our home fireside, and see and learn quite as much as some do who have actually swam in a gondola.

I cannot but envy those to whom this Shakespearian world is as yet a new and unknown world, to which they come, as I did to Venice, at sunset of a lovely April day, floating in a gondola on the Grand Canal for the first time. They may return to it again and again, as to Venice, and in some respects with increased enjoyment; but there is something in the fascination of that first experience which can never be renewed.

England and Italy are preëminently the countries of Shakespeare's plays. The scenes of fourteen of them (including the historical plays) are laid wholly or partly in England, and of eleven (including the Roman plays), wholly or partly in Italy. I count *The Tempest* among the latter because the characters are Italian, though the scene is an island not put down in any prosaic manual of geography. The other plays, twelve in number, are scattered through various lands,—Greece, Illyria, Bohemia, France, Sicily (not a part of Italy in Shakespeare's day), Denmark, etc.

Some of these are mere names. The Illyria of *Twelfth Night* and the Bohemia and Sicily of *The Winter's Tale*, for instance, might be anywhere else. In the Elizabethan age the theatres had no painted

scenery, and a sign or placard was often put up at
the back of the stage to indicate the locality, — Athens,
Rome, Venice, or whatever it might be. The sign was
the only aid to the spectator's imagination, which had
to furnish a local habitation for the name as best it
could. And so with the Messina of *Much Ado*, the
Vienna of *Measure for Measure*, the Ephesus of *The
Comedy of Errors*, and the like. They are nothing
more than names stuck up on a stage without scenery.
Transpose these names from one play to another, and
it would make no difference except in the measure of
a few lines in which they occur.

But the Italian scenes are veritably Italian. In *The
Two Gentlemen of Verona*, indeed, this local tone is not
so marked, and the poet is guilty of the blunder of
sending a ship from Verona to Milan;[1] but that is
one of the earliest plays of Shakespeare, and it is evident that he was not then so familiar with Italy as
when he wrote the later plays of which that country
is the scene.

And here the question arises, Did the poet visit
Italy? Did he ever swim in a gondola? It is not
impossible — though it seems to me, on the whole, improbable — that he may have done so. There are several years of his life after he went to London about

---

[1] It is said that there was a canal between the two cities when
Shakespeare wrote; but the allusions to the tide and to the danger
of shipwreck (i. 1. 117, ii. 3. 36) prove that he had in mind a voyage
by sea.

which we know absolutely nothing, and where he was and what he was doing can be only matter of conjecture. Critics who have been in Italy, and some who have long resided there, find it difficult to explain his minute acquaintance with the manners of the country except on the theory that he had visited it. It may be said that he got this knowledge from friends who had traveled, as some of his fellow-actors are known to have done; but, on the other hand, it is urged that such second-hand information could hardly have made him so perfectly at home in Italy that he never falls into any mistakes, even in those little matters which are rarely noted in books of travel or talked about by tourists.

In *The Merchant of Venice*, for instance (ii. 2), Old Gobbo brings a present of a "dish of doves" for Launcelot's master. "Where," asks Mr. Charles A. Brown (*Shakespeare's Autobiographical Poems*, 1858), "did the poet obtain his numerous graphic touches of national manners? Where did he learn of an old villager's coming into the city with a dish of doves as a present to his son's master? A present thus given, and of doves, is not uncommon in Italy. I myself have partaken there, with due relish, in memory of poor old Gobbo, of a dish of doves presented by the father of a servant." *The Taming of the Shrew* has many of these little Italian touches, and they are to be found in other of the Italian plays.

In *The Merchant of Venice* the very atmosphere is

Italian. In the charming fifth act, which is so refresh-
ing and restful to our feelings after the almost tragic
interest of the trial scene, like the calm and repose of
a beautiful moonlit evening after the exhaustion of an
anxious and exciting day, Portia says : —

> "This night, methinks, is but the daylight sick;
> It looks a little paler : 'tis a day
> Such as the day is when the sun is hid."

There is no such moonlight in England ; but there is
in Italy — as in New England, where we have skies as
blue and clear as bend over Venice or Florence or
Naples. To one going from England to Italy the
difference in the transparency of the atmosphere is
as striking as that in the climate or the vegetation.

But, whether Shakespeare was ever in Italy in bodily
presence, or saw its cities and its people, its skies and
its moonlight, only with the mind's eye, he takes us to
the real Italy in his plays, and not to a theatrical cari-
cature of the country. As some critic has said, the
merchant of Venice is a merchant of no other city in
the world ; and it may be added that everything in the
play is equally Venetian. And yet the strictly topo-
graphical allusions are only one or two. The Rialto
is mentioned, but it should be understood that it is
not the bridge so called, but the merchants' exchange,
which was on the Rialto, one of the islands on which
the city was built, and originally its political and commercial centre. The bridge, one end of which is on

this island (whence it gets its name), was begun in
1588 and finished in 1591, or several years before the
earliest date ascribed to the play. The exchange was
held in the open place in front of the church of San
Giacomo, a little way from the bridge. No merchants,
except humble dealers in fruit and vegetables, congregate there now, and the locality has a thoroughly plebeian character; but in the olden time it was thronged
by the Shylocks and Antonios, and their patrons and cus-
tomers, during the business hours of the day. Thomas
Coryat, in his *Crudities*, published in 1611, says: "The
Rialto, which is at the farthest side of the bridge, as
you come from St. Marks, is a most stately building,
being the Exchange of Venice, where the Venetian gentlemen and the merchants doe meete twice a day, betwixt
eleven and twelve of the clocke in the morning, and
betwixt five and sixe of the clocke in the afternoone.
This Rialto is of a goodly height, . . . adorned with
many faire walkes or open galleries, . . . and hath a
pretty quadrangular court adjoining to it." Fynes Mory-
son, in his *Ten Yeares Travell* (1617), describes it thus:
"The foure square market-place of Rialto is compassed
with publike houses, under the arches whereof, and in
the middle part lying open, the merchants meet." Archi-
tecturally it remains the same to-day, — an open square
surrounded by the arcaded buildings (like St. Mark's
Place, on a smaller scale) erected in the early part of
the sixteenth century. Near one corner of the square
is a short column of Egyptian granite, supported by a

MER. OF VEN. — 3

kneeling hunchback (" Il Gobbo di Rialto," also of the sixteenth century), from which the laws of the Republic were promulgated.

Perhaps the only other local allusion in the play, aside from the mention of gondolas, is that to " the common ferry that trades to Venice," which recognizes the insular position of the city, connected with the mainland only by ferries, as it continued to be until the building of the railway bridge in 1845. But we feel that we are in Venice all the time — Venice in the old days of its power and wealth, when the argosies of the world thronged its port, and, as Antonio says, " the trade and profit of the city consisted of all nations." It is no absurdity that suitors, not only from all parts of Italy, but from France, England, Scotland, Germany, Spain, and Morocco, are made to come as rivals for the hand of Portia, — so many Jasons in quest of the golden fleece at Belmont.

The mention of the ferry to Venice indicates that Shakespeare supposed Belmont to be on the mainland, though he probably had no definite locality in mind. We may imagine it to have been in the country westward of Venice, where there were then, as now, many villas of the Venetian nobility. This is on the direct road to Padua, about halfway between that city and Venice, which is twenty-two miles from Padua by the present railway, or twenty-six by steam tramway to Fusina and steamer from there (probably the terminus of the ancient ferry) to Venice.

THE MERCHANT OF VENICE

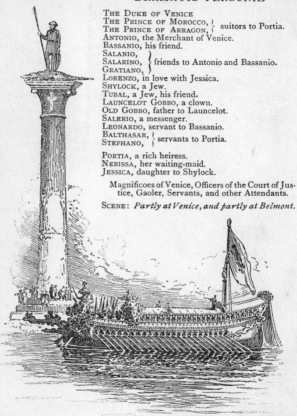

DRAMATIS PERSONÆ

THE DUKE OF VENICE
THE PRINCE OF MOROCCO, } suitors to Portia.
THE PRINCE OF ARRAGON, }
ANTONIO, the Merchant of Venice.
BASSANIO, his friend.
SALANIO, }
SALARINO, } friends to Antonio and Bassanio.
GRATIANO, }
LORENZO, in love with Jessica.
SHYLOCK, a Jew.
TUBAL, a Jew, his friend.
LAUNCELOT GOBBO, a clown.
OLD GOBBO, father to Launcelot.
SALERIO, a messenger.
LEONARDO, servant to Bassanio.
BALTHASAR, } servants to Portia.
STEPHANO, }

PORTIA, a rich heiress.
NERISSA, her waiting-maid.
JESSICA, daughter to Shylock.

Magnificoes of Venice, Officers of the Court of Justice, Gaoler, Servants, and other Attendants.

SCENE: *Partly at Venice, and partly at Belmont.*

ACT I

SCENE I. *Venice. A Street*

Enter ANTONIO, SALARINO, *and* SALANIO

Antonio. In sooth, I know not why I am so sad.
It wearies me, you say it wearies you;
But how I caught it, found it, or came by it,
What stuff 't is made of, whereof it is born,
I am to learn;
And such a want-wit sadness makes of me
That I have much ado to know myself.
   Salarino. Your mind is tossing on the ocean;
There where your argosies with portly sail,
Like signiors and rich burghers on the flood,   10

Or, as it were, the pageants of the sea,
Do overpeer the petty traffickers,
That curtsy to them, do them reverence,
As they fly by them with their woven wings.

   Salanio. Believe me, sir, had I such venture forth,
The better part of my affections would
Be with my hopes abroad.   I should be still
Plucking the grass, to know where sits the wind,
Peering in maps for ports and piers and roads;
And every object that might make me fear   20
Misfortune to my ventures, out of doubt,
Would make me sad.

   Salarino.   My wind, cooling my broth,
Would blow me to an ague when I thought
What harm a wind too great might do at sea.
I should not see the sandy hourglass run
But I should think of shallows and of flats,
And see my wealthy Andrew dock'd in sand,
Vailing her high-top lower than her ribs,
To kiss her burial.   Should I go to church
And see the holy edifice of stone,   30
And not bethink me straight of dangerous rocks,
Which, touching but my gentle vessel's side,
Would scatter all her spices on the stream,
Enrobe the roaring waters with my silks,
And, in a word, but even now worth this,
And now worth nothing?   Shall I have the thought
To think on this, and shall I lack the thought
That such a thing bechanc'd would make me sad?

But tell not me ; I know Antonio
Is sad to think upon his merchandise.   40
    Antonio. Believe me, no.   I thank my fortune for it,
My ventures are not in one bottom trusted,
Nor to one place ; nor is my whole estate
Upon the fortune of this present year.
Therefore my merchandise makes me not sad.
    Salarino. Why, then you are in love.
    Antonio.   Fie, fie !
    Salarino. Not in love neither ?   Then let us say
            you 're sad
Because you are not merry ; and 't were as easy
For you to laugh and leap, and say you 're merry
Because you are not sad.   Now, by two-headed Janus,
Nature hath fram'd strange fellows in her time :   51
Some that will evermore peep through their eyes
And laugh, like parrots, at a bag-piper ;
And other of such vinegar aspect
That they 'll not show their teeth in way of smile,
Though Nestor swear the jest be laughable.

    Enter BASSANIO, LORENZO, *and* GRATIANO

    Salanio. Here comes Bassanio, your most noble
            kinsman,
Gratiano, and Lorenzo.   Fare ye well ;
We leave you now with better company.
    Salarino. I would have stay'd till I had made you
            merry,   60
If worthier friends had not prevented me.

Antonio. Your worth is very dear in my regard.
I take it, your own business calls on you,
And you embrace the occasion to depart.

Salarino. Good morrow, my good lords.

Bassanio. Good signiors both, when shall we laugh?
    Say, when?
You grow exceeding strange; must it be so?

Salarino. We'll make our leisures to attend on yours.
                    [*Exeunt Salarino and Salanio.*

Lorenzo. My Lord Bassanio, since you've found
    Antonio,
We two will leave you; but at dinner-time,   70
I pray you, have in mind where we must meet.

Bassanio. I will not fail you.

Gratiano. You look not well, Signior Antonio.
You have too much respect upon the world;
They lose it that do buy it with much care.
Believe me, you are marvellously chang'd.

Antonio. I hold the world but as the world, Gratiano,
A stage where every man must play a part,
And mine a sad one.

Gratiano.   Let me play the fool;
With mirth and laughter let old wrinkles come,   80
And let my liver rather heat with wine
Than my heart cool with mortifying groans.
Why should a man whose blood is warm within
Sit like his grandsire cut in alabaster?
Sleep when he wakes, and creep into the jaundice
By being peevish? I tell thee what, Antonio, —

I love thee, and it is my love that speaks, —
There are a sort of men whose visages
Do cream and mantle like a standing pond,
And do a wilful stillness entertain,　　　　　90
With purpose to be dress'd in an opinion
Of wisdom, gravity, profound conceit;
As who should say, 'I am Sir Oracle,
And when I ope my lips let no dog bark!'
O my Antonio, I do know of these
That therefore only are reputed wise
For saying nothing; when, I am very sure,
If they should speak, would almost damn those ears
Which, hearing them, would call their brothers fools.
I'll tell thee more of this another time;　　　100
But fish not, with this melancholy bait,
For this fool gudgeon, this opinion. —
Come, good Lorenzo. — Fare ye well awhile;
I'll end my exhortation after dinner.

   Lorenzo.　Well, we will leave you then till dinner-time.
I must be one of these same dumb wise men,
For Gratiano never lets me speak.

   Gratiano.　Well, keep me company but two years moe,
Thou shalt not know the sound of thine own tongue.

   Antonio.　Farewell; I'll grow a talker for this gear.

   Gratiano.　Thanks, i' faith; for silence is only commendable　　　　　　　　　　　　　　　　　111
In a neat's tongue dried.

               [*Exeunt Gratiano and Lorenzo.*

   Antonio.　Is that any thing now?

Bassanio. Gratiano speaks an infinite deal of nothing,
more than any man in all Venice. His reasons are as
two grains of wheat hid in two bushels of chaff ; you
shall seek all day ere you find them, and when you have
them they are not worth the search.

Antonio. Well, tell me now, what lady is the same
To whom you swore a secret pilgrimage,   120
That you to-day promis'd to tell me of ?

Bassanio. 'T is not unknown to you, Antonio,
How much I have disabled mine estate,
By something showing a mere swelling port
Than my faint means would grant continuance ;
Nor do I now make moan to be abridg'd
From such a noble rate, but my chief care
Is to come fairly off from the great debts
Wherein my time, something too prodigal,
Hath left me gag'd.   To you, Antonio,   130
I owe the most, in money and in love ;
And from your love I have a warranty
To unburthen all my plots and purposes,
How to get clear of all the debts I owe.

Antonio. I pray you, good Bassanio, let me know it ;
And if it stand, as you yourself still do,
Within the eye of honour, be assur'd,
My purse, my person, my extremest means,
Lie all unlock'd to your occasions.

Bassanio. In my school days, when I had lost one
    shaft,   140
I shot his fellow of the selfsame flight

The selfsame way, with more advised watch,
To find the other forth ; and by adventuring both
I oft found both.   I urge this childhood proof
Because what follows is pure innocence.
I owe you much, and, like a wilful youth,
That which I owe is lost ; but if you please
To shoot another arrow that self way
Which you did shoot the first, I do not·doubt,
As I will watch the aim, or to find both   150
Or bring your latter hazard back again,
And thankfully rest debtor for the first.

    Antonio. You know me well, and herein spend but time
To wind about my love with circumstance ;
And, out of doubt, you do me now more wrong
In making question of my uttermost
Than if you had made waste of all I have.
Then do but say to me what I should do,
That in your knowledge may by me be done,
And I am prest unto it ; therefore speak.   160

    Bassanio. In Belmont is a lady richly left ;
And she is fair and, fairer than that word,
Of wondrous virtues.   Sometimes from her eyes
I did receive fair speechless messages.
Her name is Portia, nothing undervalued
To Cato's daughter, Brutus' Portia.
Nor is the wide world ignorant of her worth,
For the four winds blow in from every coast
Renowned suitors ; and her sunny locks
Hang on her temples like a golden fleece,   170

Which makes her seat of Belmont Colchos' strand,
And many Jasons come in quest of her.
O my Antonio, had I but the means
To hold a rival place with one of them,
I have a mind presages me such thrift
That I should questionless be fortunate.

Antonio. Thou know'st that all my fortunes are at sea ;
Neither have I money nor commodity
To raise a present sum.   Therefore go forth ;
Try what my credit can in Venice do.   180
That shall be rack'd, even to the uttermost,
To furnish thee to Belmont, to fair Portia.
Go, presently inquire, and so will I,
Where money is, and I no question make
To have it of my trust or for my sake.   *[Exeunt.*

SCENE II.   *Belmont.   A Room in Portia's House*

Enter PORTIA *and* NERISSA

Portia. By my troth, Nerissa, my little body is
aweary of this great world.

Nerissa. You would be, sweet madam, if your
miseries were in the same abundance as your good
fortunes are ; and yet, for aught I see, they are as sick
that surfeit with too much as they that starve with
nothing.   It is no mean happiness, therefore, to be
seated in the mean ; superfluity comes sooner by
white hairs, but competency lives longer.

Portia. Good sentences, and well pronounced.   10

Nerissa. They would be better if well followed.

Portia. If to do were as easy as to know what were good to do, chapels had been churches, and poor men's cottages princes' palaces. It is a good divine that follows his own instructions; I can easier teach twenty what were good to be done than be one of the twenty to follow mine own teaching. The brain may devise laws for the blood, but a hot temper leaps o'er a cold decree; such a hare is madness, the youth, to skip o'er the meshes of good counsel, the cripple. But this reasoning is not in the fashion to choose me a husband. — O me, the word 'choose!' I may neither choose whom I would, nor refuse whom I dislike; so is the will of a living daughter curbed by the will of a dead father. Is it not hard, Nerissa, that I cannot choose one, nor refuse none?

Nerissa. Your father was ever virtuous, and holy men at their death have good inspirations; therefore the lottery that he hath devised in these three chests of gold, silver, and lead — whereof who chooses his meaning chooses you — will, no doubt, never be chosen by any rightly but one who you shall rightly love. But what warmth is there in your affection towards any of these princely suitors that are already come?

Portia. I pray thee, over-name them, and as thou namest them I will describe them; and, according to my description, level at my affection.

Nerissa. First, there is the Neapolitan prince.

Portia. Ay, that 's a colt indeed, for he doth 40
nothing but talk of his horse ; and he makes it a
great appropriation to his own good parts that he can
shoe him himself.

Nerissa. Then is there the County Palatine.

Portia. He doth nothing but frown, as who should
say, ' An you will not have me, choose.' He hears
merry tales, and smiles not ; I fear he will prove the
weeping philosopher when he grows old, being so
full of unmannerly sadness in his youth. I had
rather to be married to a death's-head with a bone 50
in his mouth than to either of these. God defend
me from these two!

Nerissa. How say you by the French lord, Mon-
sieur Le Bon ?

Portia. God made him, and therefore let him pass
for a man. In truth, I know it is a sin to be a
mocker ; but he ! why, he hath a horse better than
the Neapolitan's, a better bad habit of frowning than
the Count Palatine. He is every man in no man ;
if a throstle sing, he falls straight a-capering ; he 60
will fence with his own shadow. If I should marry
him, I should marry twenty husbands. If he would
despise me, I would forgive him ; for if he love me
to madness, I shall never requite him.

Nerissa. What say you then to Falconbridge, the
young baron of England ?

Portia. You know I say nothing to him, for he
understands not me, nor I him ; he hath neither

Latin, French, nor Italian, and you will come into
the court and swear that I have a poor pennyworth 70
in the English.   He is a proper man's picture ; but,
alas ! who can converse with a dumb show ?   How
oddly he is suited !   I think he bought his doublet
in Italy, his round hose in France, his bonnet in
Germany, and his behaviour every where.

Nerissa. What think you of the Scottish lord, his
neighbour ?

Portia. That he hath a neighbourly charity in
him ; for he borrowed a box of the ear of the English-
man, and swore he would pay him again when he 80
was able.   I think the Frenchman became his surety
and sealed under for another.

Nerissa. How like you the young German, the
Duke of Saxony's nephew ?

Portia. Very vilely in the morning when he is
sober, and most vilely in the afternoon when he
is drunk.   When he is best, he is a little worse than
a man ; and when he is worst, he is little better than
a beast.   An the worst fall that ever fell, I hope I
shall make shift to go without him.   90

Nerissa. If he should offer to choose, and choose
the right casket, you should refuse to perform your
father's will if you should refuse to accept him.

Portia. Therefore, for fear of the worst, I pray
thee, set a deep glass of Rhenish wine on the contrary casket ; for if the devil be within and that
temptation without, I know he will choose it.   I will

do any thing, Nerissa, ere I will be married to a sponge.

Nerissa. You need not fear, lady, the having any 100 of these lords.   They have acquainted me with their determinations; which is, indeed, to return to their home, and to trouble you with no more suit, unless you may be won by some other sort than your father's imposition depending on the caskets.

Portia. If I live to be as old as Sibylla, I will die as chaste as Diana, unless I be obtained by the manner of my father's will.   I am glad this parcel of wooers are so reasonable, for there is not one among them but I dote on his very absence; and 110 I wish them a fair departure.

Nerissa. Do you not remember, lady, in your father's time, a Venetian, a scholar and a soldier, that came hither in company of the Marquis of Montferrat?

Portia. Yes, yes, it was Bassanio; as I think, so was he called.

Nerissa. True, madam; he, of all the men that ever my foolish eyes looked upon, was the best deserving a fair lady.   120

Portia. I remember him well, and I remember him worthy of thy praise.

Enter a Servant

Servant. The four strangers seek for you, madam, to take their leave; and there is a forerunner come

from a fifth, the Prince of Morocco, who brings word
the prince his master will be here to-night.

Portia. If I could bid the fifth welcome with so
good heart as I can bid the other four farewell, I
should be glad of his approach; if he have the condition of a saint and the complexion of a devil, I had 130
rather he should shrive me than wive me.
Come, Nerissa. — Sirrah, go before. —
Whiles we shut the gates upon one wooer, another
      knocks at the door.   [*Exeunt.*

SCENE III.   *Venice.   A Public Place*

Enter BASSANIO *and* SHYLOCK

Shylock. Three thousand ducats, — well.

Bassanio. Ay, sir, for three months.

Shylock. For three months, — well.

Bassanio. For the which, as I told you, Antonio
shall be bound.

Shylock. Antonio shall become bound, — well.

Bassanio. May you stead me? Will you pleasure
me? Shall I know your answer?

Shylock. Three thousand ducats for three months,
and Antonio bound.   10

Bassanio. Your answer to that.

Shylock. Antonio is a good man.

Bassanio. Have you heard any imputation to the
contrary?

Shylock. Ho, no, no, no, no; my meaning, in say-

ing he is a good man, is to have you understand me
that he is sufficient. Yet his means are in supposition: he hath an argosy bound to Tripolis, another
to the Indies; I understand, moreover, upon the
Rialto, he hath a third at Mexico, a fourth for Eng- 20
land, and other ventures he hath, squandered abroad.
But ships are but boards, sailors but men: there
be land-rats and water-rats, land-thieves and water-
thieves, — I mean pirates; and then there is the
peril of waters, winds, and rocks. The man is, notwithstanding, sufficient. Three thousand ducats, —
I think I may take his bond.

Bassanio. Be assured you may.

Shylock. I will be assured I may; and that I may
be assured I will bethink me. May I speak with 30
Antonio?

Bassanio. If it please you to dine with us.

Shylock. Yes, to smell pork; to eat of the habitation which your prophet, the Nazarite, conjured the
devil into. I will buy with you, sell with you, talk
with you, walk with you, and so following; but I will
not eat with you, drink with you, nor pray with you.
— What news on the Rialto? — Who is he comes
here?

Enter ANTONIO

Bassanio. This is Signior Antonio.   40

Shylock. [*Aside*] How like a fawning publican he
        looks!
I hate him for he is a Christian,

But more for that, in low simplicity,
He lends out money gratis and brings down
The rate of usance here with us in Venice.
If I can catch him once upon the hip,
I will feed fat the ancient grudge I bear him.
He hates our sacred nation ; and he rails,
Even there where merchants most do congregate,
On me, my bargains, and my well-won thrift, 50
Which he calls interest.   Cursed be my tribe
If I forgive him !

   Bassanio.   Shylock, do you hear ?

   Shylock. I am debating of my present store ;
And, by the near guess of my memory,
I cannot instantly raise up the gross
Of full three thousand ducats.   What of that ?
Tubal, a wealthy Hebrew of my tribe,
Will furnish me.   But soft ! how many months
Do you desire? — [*To Antonio*] Rest you fair, good
      signior ;
Your worship was the last man in our mouths. 60

   Antonio. Shylock, albeit I neither lend nor borrow
By taking nor by giving of excess,
Yet, to supply the ripe wants of my friend,
I 'll break a custom. — Is he yet possess'd
How much you would ?

   Shylock.   Ay, ay, three thousand ducats.

   Antonio. And for three months.

   Shylock. I had forgot, — three months ; you told me so.
Well then, your bond ; and let me see — but hear you :

Methought you said you neither lend nor borrow
Upon advantage.

    Antonio.   I do never use it.   70

    Shylock. When Jacob graz'd his uncle Laban's
    sheep —
This Jacob from our holy Abram was,
As his wise mother wrought in his behalf,
The third possessor; ay, he was the third —

    Antonio. And what of him? did he take interest?

    Shylock. No, not take interest, not, as you would say,
Directly interest; mark what Jacob did.
When Laban and himself were compromis'd
That all the eanlings which were streak'd and pied
Should fall as Jacob's hire,   80
The skilful shepherd pill'd me certain wands
And stuck them up before the fulsome ewes,
Who, then conceiving, did in eaning time
Fall parti-colour'd lambs; and those were Jacob's.
This was a way to thrive, and he was blest;
And thrift is blessing, if men steal it not.

    Antonio. This was a venture, sir, that Jacob serv'd for;
A thing not in his power to bring to pass,
But sway'd and fashion'd by the hand of heaven.
Was this inserted to make interest good?   90
Or is your gold and silver ewes and rams?

    Shylock. I cannot tell; I make it breed as fast. —
But note me, signior.

    Antonio.   Mark you this, Bassanio,
The devil can cite Scripture for his purpose.

An evil soul, producing holy witness,
Is like a villain with a smiling cheek,
A goodly apple rotten at the heart.
O, what a goodly outside falsehood hath!
　　Shylock.　Three thousand ducats, — 't is a good round
　　　　sum.　　　　　　　　　　　　　　　　　　　99
Three months from twelve, — then, let me see the rate.
　　Antonio.　Well, Shylock, shall we be beholding to you?
　　Shylock.　Signior Antonio, many a time and oft,
In the Rialto, you have rated me
About my moneys and my usances;
Still have I borne it with a patient shrug,
For sufferance is the badge of all our tribe.
You call me misbeliever, cut-throat dog,
And spet upon my Jewish gaberdine,
And all for use of that which is mine own.
Well then, it now appears you need my help.　　　110
Go to, then; you come to me, and you say,
' Shylock, we would have moneys.'　You say so,
You, that did void your rheum upon my beard,
And foot me as you spurn a stranger cur
Over your threshold; moneys is your suit.
What should I say to you?　Should I not say,
' Hath a dog money?　Is it possible
A cur should lend three thousand ducats?'　Or
Shall I bend low, and in a bondman's key,
With bated breath and whispering humbleness,　　　120
Say this:
' Fair sir, you spet on me on Wednesday last;

You spurn'd me such a day; another time
You call'd me dog; and for these courtesies
I 'll lend you thus much moneys?'

  Antonio. I am as like to call thee so again,
To spet on thee again, to spurn thee too.
If thou wilt lend this money, lend it not
As to thy friends; for when did friendship take
A breed of barren metal of his friend?   130
But lend it rather to thine enemy,
Who if he break, thou mayst with better face
Exact the penalty.

  Shylock.   Why, look you, how you storm!
I would be friends with you, and have your love,
Forget the shames that you have stain'd me with,
Supply your present wants, and take no doit
Of usance for my moneys, and you 'll not hear me.
This is kind I offer.

  Bassanio. This were kindness.

  Shylock.   This kindness will I show.
Go with me to a notary; seal me there   140
Your single bond; and, in a merry sport,
If you repay me not on such a day,
In such a place, such sum or sums as are
Express'd in the condition, let the forfeit
Be nominated for an equal pound
Of your fair flesh, to be cut off and taken
In what part of your body pleaseth me.

  Antonio. Content, i' faith; I 'll seal to such a bond,
And say there is much kindness in the Jew.   149

Bassanio. You shall not seal to such a bond for me ;
I 'll rather dwell in my necessity.

Antonio. Why, fear not, man ; I will not forfeit it.
Within these two months — that 's a month before
This bond expires — I do expect return
Of thrice three times the value of this bond.

Shylock. O father Abram ! what these Christians are
Whose own hard dealings teaches them suspect
The thoughts of others ! — Pray you, tell me this :
If he should break his day, what should I gain
By the exaction of the forfeiture ?   160
A pound of man's flesh, taken from a man,
Is not so estimable, profitable neither,
As flesh of muttons, beefs, or goats.   I say,
To buy his favour I extend this friendship.
If he will take it, so ; if not, adieu ;
And, for my love, I pray you wrong me not.

Antonio. Yes, Shylock, I will seal unto this bond.

Shylock. Then meet me forthwith at the notary's.
Give him direction for this merry bond,
And I will go and purse the ducats straight,   170
See to my house, left in the fearful guard
Of an unthrifty knave, and presently
I will be with you.   [*Exit.*

Antonio.   Hie thee, gentle Jew. —
The Hebrew will turn Christian ; he grows kind.

Bassanio. I like not fair terms and a villain's mind.

Antonio. Come on : in this there can be no dismay ;
My ships come home a month before the day.   [*Exeunt.*

VENICE

ACT II

Scene I. *Belmont.   A Room in Portia's House*

Flourish of Cornets.   Enter the Prince of Morocco
and his train; Portia, Nerissa, *and others
attending.*

Morocco. Mislike me not for my complexion,
The shadow'd livery of the burnish'd sun,
To whom I am a neighbour and near bred.
Bring me the fairest creature northward born,
Where Phœbus' fire scarce thaws the icicles,
And let us make incision for your love,
To prove whose blood is reddest, his or mine.
I tell thee, lady, this aspect of mine
Hath fear'd the valiant; by my love, I swear
The best-regarded virgins of our clime   10

Have lov'd it too.   I would not change this hue,
Except to steal your thoughts, my gentle queen.

 Portia. In terms of choice I am not solely led
By nice direction of a maiden's eyes ;
Besides, the lottery of my destiny
Bars me the right of voluntary choosing ;
But if my father had not scanted me,
And hedg'd me by his wit, to yield myself
His wife who wins me by that means I told you,
Yourself, renowned prince, then stood as fair   20
As any comer I have look'd on yet,
For my affection.

 Morocco.   Even for that I thank you ;
Therefore, I pray you, lead me to the caskets
To try my fortune.   By this scimitar,
That slew the Sophy and a Persian prince
That won three fields of Sultan Solyman,
I would o'er-stare the sternest eyes that look,
Outbrave the heart most daring on the earth,
Pluck the young sucking cubs from the she-bear,
Yea, mock the lion when he roars for prey,   30
To win thee, lady.   But, alas the while !
If Hercules and Lichas play at dice
Which is the better man, the greater throw
May turn by fortune from the weaker hand.
So is Alcides beaten by his page ;
And so may I, blind Fortune leading me,
Miss that which one unworthier may attain,
And die with grieving.

Portia.   You must take your chance,
And either not attempt to choose at all,
Or swear, before you choose, if you choose wrong   40
Never to speak to lady afterward
In way of marriage ; therefore be advis'd.

Morocco. Nor will not.   Come, bring me unto my
    chance.

Portia.   First, forward to the temple ; after dinner
Your hazard shall be made.

Morocco.   Good fortune then,
To make me blest or cursed'st among men !

                        [*Cornets, and exeunt.*

SCENE II.   *Venice.   A Street*

Enter LAUNCELOT

Launcelot.   Certainly my conscience will serve me
to run from this Jew my master.   The fiend is at mine
elbow and tempts me, saying to me, 'Gobbo, Launcelot Gobbo, good Launcelot,' or 'good Gobbo,' or
'good Launcelot Gobbo, use your legs, take the start,
run away.'   My conscience says, 'No ; take heed,
honest Launcelot ; take heed, honest Gobbo,' or, as
aforesaid, 'honest Launcelot Gobbo ; do not run ;
scorn running with thy heels.'   Well, the most cour-
ageous fiend bids me pack : 'Via !' says the fiend ;   10
'away !' says the fiend ; 'for the heavens, rouse up
a brave mind,' says the fiend, 'and run.'   Well, my

conscience, hanging about the neck of my heart,
says very wisely to me, 'My honest friend Launcelot, being an honest man's son,'— or rather an
honest woman's son, — well, my conscience says,
'Launcelot, budge not.' 'Budge,' says the fiend.
'Budge not,' says my conscience. 'Conscience,'
say I, 'you counsel well;' 'Fiend,' say I, 'you
counsel well.' To be ruled by my conscience, I 20
should stay with the Jew my master, who, God bless
the mark, is a kind of devil; and, to run away from
the Jew, I should be ruled by the fiend, who, saving
your reverence, is the devil himself. Certainly the
Jew is the very devil incarnation; and, in my conscience, my conscience is a kind of hard conscience,
to offer to counsel me to stay with the Jew. The
fiend gives the more friendly counsel. I will run,
fiend; my heels are at your commandment; I will
run.   30

Enter Old GOBBO, *with a basket*

Gobbo. Master young man, you! I pray you,
which is the way to master Jew's?

Launcelot. [*Aside*] O heavens! this is my true-
begotten father, who, being more than sand-blind,
high-gravel-blind, knows me not. — I will try confusions with him.

Gobbo. Master young gentleman, I pray you,
which is the way to master Jew's?

Launcelot. Turn up on your right hand at the next
turning, but at the next turning of all, on your left; 40

marry, at the very next turning, turn of no hand, but turn down indirectly to the Jew's house.

Gobbo. By God's sonties, 't will be a hard way to hit. Can you tell me whether one Launcelot, that dwells with him, dwell with him or no?

Launcelot. Talk you of young Master Launcelot? —[*Aside*] Mark me now; now will I raise the waters. —[*To him*] Talk you of young Master Launcelot?

Gobbo. No master, sir, but a poor man's son; his 50 father, though I say 't, is an honest exceeding poor man, and, God be thanked, well to live.

Launcelot. Well, let his father be what a' will, we talk of young Master Launcelot.

Gobbo. Your worship's friend and Launcelot.

Launcelot. But I pray you, ergo, old man, ergo, I beseech you, talk you of young Master Launcelot?

Gobbo. Of Launcelot, an 't please your mastership.

Launcelot. Ergo, Master Launcelot. Talk not of Master Launcelot, father; for the young gentleman 60 — according to fates and destinies and such odd sayings, the sisters three and such branches of learning — is indeed deceased, or, as you would say in plain terms, gone to heaven.

Gobbo. Marry, God forbid! the boy was the very staff of my age, my very prop.

Launcelot. [*Aside*] Do I look like a cudgel or a hovel-post, a staff or a prop? [*To him*] Do you know me, father?

Gobbo. Alack the day! I know you not, young 70
gentleman; but, I pray you, tell me, is my boy —
God rest his soul! — alive or dead?

Launcelot. Do you not know me, father?

Gobbo. Alack, sir, I am sand-blind; I know you
not.

Launcelot. Nay, indeed, if you had your eyes, you
might fail of the knowing me; it is a wise father that
knows his own child. Well, old man, I will tell you
news of your son. [*Kneels.*] Give me your blessing: truth will come to light; murther cannot be 80
hid long; a man's son may, but in the end truth
will out.

Gobbo. Pray you, sir, stand up. I am sure you
are not Launcelot, my boy.

Launcelot. Pray you, let's have no more fooling
about it, but give me your blessing; I am Launcelot,
your boy that was, your son that is, your child that
shall be.

Gobbo. I cannot think you are my son.

Launcelot. I know not what I shall think of that; 90
but I am Launcelot, the Jew's man, and I am sure
Margery your wife is my mother.

Gobbo. Her name is Margery, indeed; I 'll be
sworn, if thou be Launcelot, thou art mine own flesh
and blood. Lord worshipped might he be! what a
beard hast thou got! thou hast got more hair on thy
chin than Dobbin my fill-horse has on his tail.

Launcelot. It should seem, then, that Dobbin's tail

grows backward; I am sure he had more hair of his
tail than I have of my face, when I last saw him. 100

Gobbo. Lord! how art thou changed! How dost
thou and thy master agree? I have brought him a
present. How gree you now?

Launcelot. Well, well; but, for mine own part, as
I have set up my rest to run away, so I will not rest
till I have run some ground. My master's a very
Jew; give him a present! give him a halter. I am
famished in his service; you may tell every finger I
have with my ribs. Father, I am glad you are come.
Give me your present to one Master Bassanio, who 110
indeed gives rare new liveries; if I serve not him, I
will run as far as God has any ground.—O rare
fortune! here comes the man.—To him, father;
for I am a Jew if I serve the Jew any longer.

Enter BASSANIO, *with* LEONARDO *and other followers*

Bassanio. You may do so; but let it be so hasted
that supper be ready at the farthest by five of the
clock. See these letters delivered; put the liveries
to making, and desire Gratiano to come anon to
my lodging.   [*Exit a Servant.*

Launcelot. To him, father.   120

Gobbo. God bless your worship!

Bassanio. Gramercy! wouldst thou aught with me?

Gobbo. Here's my son, sir, a poor boy,—

Launcelot. Not a poor boy, sir, but the rich Jew's
man; that would, sir, as my father shall specify,—

Gobbo. He hath a great infection, sir, as one
would say, to serve —

Launcelot. Indeed, the short and the long is, I
serve the Jew, and have a desire, as my father shall
specify, —   130

Gobbo. His master and he, saving your worship's
reverence, are scarce cater-cousins —

Launcelot. To be brief, the very truth is, that the
Jew, having done me wrong, doth cause me, as my
father, being, I hope, an old man, shall frutify unto
you, —

Gobbo. I have here a dish of doves that I would
bestow upon your worship; and my suit is —

Launcelot. In very brief, the suit is impertinent
to myself, as your worship shall know by this honest 140
old man; and, though I say it, though old man, yet,
poor man, my father.

Bassanio. One speak for both. — What would you?

Launcelot. Serve you, sir.

Gobbo. That is the very defect of the matter, sir.

Bassanio. I know thee well; thou hast obtain'd
         thy suit.
Shylock thy master spoke with me this day,
And hath preferr'd thee; if it be preferment
To leave a rich Jew's service, to become
The follower of so poor a gentleman.   150

Launcelot. The old proverb is very well parted
between my master Shylock and you, sir; you have
the grace of God, sir, and he hath enough.

Bassanio. Thou speak'st it well. — Go, father,
 with thy son. —
Take leave of thy old master, and inquire
My lodging out. — Give him a livery [*To his followers.*
More guarded than his fellows'; see it done.

Launcelot. Father, in. — I cannot get a service, no;
I have ne'er a tongue in my head. — Well, if any
man in Italy have a fairer table which doth offer 160
to swear upon a book! — I shall have good fortune.
— Go to, here's a simple line of life! here's a small
trifle of wives: alas! fifteen wives is nothing! aleven
widows and nine maids is a simple coming-in for one
man; and then to scape drowning thrice, and to be
in peril of my life with the edge of a feather-bed,
— here are simple scapes. Well, if Fortune be a
woman, she's a good wench for this gear. — Father,
come; I'll take my leave of the Jew in the twinkling
of an eye. [*Exeunt Launcelot and Old Gobbo.*

Bassanio. I pray thee, good Leonardo, think on
 this. 171
These things being bought and orderly bestow'd,
Return in haste, for I do feast to-night
My best-esteem'd acquaintance; hie thee, go.

Leonardo. My best endeavours shall be done
 herein.

   Enter GRATIANO

Gratiano. Where is your master?
Leonardo.   Yonder, sir, he walks. [*Exit.*
Gratiano. Signior Bassanio!

Bassanio. Gratiano!

Gratiano. I have a suit to you.

Bassanio. You have obtain'd it.

Gratiano. You must not deny me. I must go 180
with you to Belmont.

Bassanio. Why, then you must. But hear thee,
   Gratiano:
Thou art too wild, too rude, and bold of voice, —
Parts that become thee happily enough
And in such eyes as ours appear not faults;
But where they are not known, why, there they show
Something too liberal. Pray thee, take pain
To allay with some cold drops of modesty
Thy skipping spirit, lest through thy wild behaviour
I be misconstrued in the place I go to,   190
And lose my hopes.

Gratiano. Signior Bassanio, hear me:
If I do not put on a sober habit,
Talk with respect, and swear but now and then,
Wear prayer-books in my pocket, look demurely,
Nay more, while grace is saying, hood mine eyes
Thus with my hat, and sigh, and say ' amen,'
Use all the observance of civility,
Like one well studied in a sad ostent
To please his grandam, never trust me more.

Bassanio. Well, we shall see your bearing.   200

Gratiano. Nay, but I bar to-night; you shall not
   gauge me
By what we do to-night.

Bassanio.   No, that were pity;
I would entreat you rather to put on
Your boldest suit of mirth, for we have friends
That purpose merriment.   But fare you well;
I have some business.

   Gratiano. And I must to Lorenzo and the rest;
But we will visit you at supper-time.   [*Exeunt.*

SCENE III.   *The Same.   A Room in Shylock's House*

Enter JESSICA *and* LAUNCELOT

   Jessica. I am sorry thou wilt leave my father so;
Our house is hell, and thou, a merry devil,
Didst rob it of some taste of tediousness.
But fare thee well; there is a ducat for thee.
And, Launcelot, soon at supper shalt thou see
Lorenzo, who is thy new master's guest.
Give him this letter; do it secretly.
And so farewell; I would not have my father
See me in talk with thee.

   Launcelot. Adieu! tears exhibit my tongue.   Most 10
beautiful pagan, most sweet Jew, adieu! these foolish drops do somewhat drown my manly spirit;
adieu!

   Jessica. Farewell, good Launcelot. —

                              [*Exit Launcelot.*

Alack, what heinous sin is it in me
To be asham'd to be my father's child!
But though I am a daughter to his blood,

I am not to his manners.   O Lorenzo,
If thou keep promise, I shall end this strife,
Become a Christian and thy loving wife !   [*Exit.* 20

SCENE IV. *The Same.   A Street*

Enter GRATIANO, LORENZO, SALARINO, *and* SALANIO

Lorenzo. Nay, we will slink away in supper-time,
Disguise us at my lodging, and return,
All in an hour.
  Gratiano. We have not made good preparation.
  Salarino. We have not spoke us yet of torch-
      bearers.
  Salanio. 'T is vile unless it may be quaintly
      order'd,
And better, in my mind, not undertook.
  Lorenzo. 'T is now but four o'clock; we have two
          hours
To furnish us. —

Enter LAUNCELOT, *with a letter*

          Friend Launcelot, what 's the news ?
  Launcelot. An it shall please you to break up 10
this, it shall seem to signify.
  Lorenzo. I know the hand.   In faith, 't is a fair
      hand ;
And whiter than the paper it writ on
Is the fair hand that writ.

Gratiano.   Love-news, in faith.

Launcelot. By your leave, sir.

Lorenzo. Whither goest thou?

Launcelot. Marry, sir, to bid my old master the Jew to sup to-night with my new master the Christian.

Lorenzo. Hold here, take this. — Tell gentle Jessica
I will not fail her; — speak it privately.   20
Go. — Gentlemen,   [*Exit Launcelot.*
Will you prepare you for this masque to-night?
I am provided of a torch-bearer.

Salarino. Ay, marry, I 'll be gone about it straight.

Salanio. And so will I.

Lorenzo.   Meet me and Gratiano
At Gratiano's lodging some hour hence.

Salarino. 'T is good we do so.

                    [*Exeunt Salarino and Salanio.*

Gratiano. Was not that letter from fair Jessica?

Lorenzo. I must needs tell thee all.   She hath directed
How I shall take her from her father's house,   30
What gold and jewels she is furnish'd with,
What page's suit she hath in readiness.
If e'er the Jew her father come to heaven,
It will be for his gentle daughter's sake;
And never dare Misfortune cross her foot,
Unless she do it under this excuse,
That she is issue to a faithless Jew.
Come, go with me; peruse this as thou goest.
Fair Jessica shall be my torch-bearer.   [*Exeunt.*

SCENE V.   *The Same.   Before Shylock's House*

Enter SHYLOCK *and* LAUNCELOT

Shylock. Well, thou shalt see; thy eyes shall be
      thy judge,
The difference of old Shylock and Bassanio. —
What, Jessica! — thou shalt not gormandize,
As thou hast done with me, — what, Jessica! —
And sleep and snore, and rend apparel out —
Why, Jessica, I say!
      Launcelot.   Why, Jessica!
      Shylock. Who bids thee call?   I do not bid thee
            call.
      Launcelot. Your worship was wont to tell me I
could do nothing without bidding.

Enter JESSICA

Jessica. Call you? what is your will?   10
      Shylock. I am bid forth to supper, Jessica;
There are my keys. — But wherefore should I go?
I am not bid for love, they flatter me;
But yet I 'll go in hate, to feed upon
The prodigal Christian. — Jessica, my girl,
Look to my house. — I am right loath to go;
There is some ill a-brewing towards my rest,
For I did dream of money-bags to-night.
      Launcelot. I beseech you, sir, go; my young
master doth expect your reproach.   20
      Shylock. So do I his.

Launcelot. And they have conspired together ; —
I will not say you shall see a masque ; but if you do,
then it was not for nothing that my nose fell a-bleed-
ing on Black-Monday last at six o'clock i' the morning, falling out that year on Ash-Wednesday was four
year in the afternoon.

Shylock. What ! are there masques ? — Hear you
    me, Jessica :

Lock up my doors ; and when you hear the drum
And the vile squealing of the wry-neck'd fife,   30
Clamber not you up to the casements then,
Nor thrust your head into the public street
To gaze on Christian fools with varnish'd faces,
But stop my house's ears, — I mean my casements ;
Let not the sound of shallow foppery enter
My sober house. — By Jacob's staff, I swear,
I have no mind of feasting forth to-night ;
But I will go. — Go you before me, sirrah ;
Say I will come.

Launcelot. I will go before, sir. — Mistress, look out
at window, for all this :   41

> There will come a Christian by,
> Will be worth a Jewess' eye.   [*Exit.*

Shylock. What says that fool of Hagar's offspring, ha ?

Jessica. His words were ' Farewell, mistress ; ' noth-
    ing else.

Shylock. The patch is kind enough, but a huge
    feeder ;

Snail-slow in profit, and he sleeps by day

More than the wild-cat.   Drones hive not with me;
Therefore I part with him, and part with him
To one that I would have him help to waste   50
His borrow'd purse. — Well, Jessica, go in;
Perhaps I will return immediately.
Do as I bid you; shut doors after you.
Fast bind, fast find;
A proverb never stale in thrifty mind.   [*Exit.*

   Jessica. Farewell; and if my fortune be not crost,
I have a father, you a daughter, lost.   [*Exit.*

SCENE VI. *The Same*

Enter GRATIANO *and* SALARINO, *masqued*

   Gratiano. This is the pent-house under which Lorenzo
Desir'd us to make stand.

   Salarino.   His hour is almost past.

   Gratiano. And it is marvel he outdwells his hour,
For lovers ever run before the clock.

   Salarino. O, ten times faster Venus' pigeons fly
To seal love's bonds new-made than they are wont
To keep obliged faith unforfeited!

   Gratiano. That ever holds.   Who riseth from a feast
With that keen appetite that he sits down?
Where is the horse that doth untread again   10
His tedious measures with the unbated fire
That he did pace them first?   All things that are
Are with more spirit chased than enjoy'd.
How like a younger or a prodigal,

The scarfed bark puts from her native bay,
Hugg'd and embraced by the strumpet wind!
How like the prodigal doth she return,
With over-weather'd ribs and ragged sails,
Lean, rent, and beggar'd by the strumpet wind!

    Salarino. Here comes Lorenzo. — More of this
       hereafter.   20

Enter LORENZO

    Lorenzo. Sweet friends, your patience for my long
       abode;
Not I, but my affairs, have made you wait.
When you shall please to play the thieves for wives,
I 'll watch as long for you then. — Approach;
Here dwells my father Jew. — Ho! who 's within?

Enter JESSICA, *above, in boy's clothes*

    Jessica. Who are you? Tell me, for more certainty,
Albeit I 'll swear that I do know your tongue.
    Lorenzo. Lorenzo, and thy love.
    Jessica. Lorenzo, certain; and my love indeed,
For who love I so much? And now who knows   30
But you, Lorenzo, whether I am yours?
    Lorenzo. Heaven and thy thoughts are witness that
       thou art.
    Jessica. Here, catch this casket; it is worth the pains.
I am glad 't is night, you do not look on me,
For I am much asham'd of my exchange.
But love is blind, and lovers cannot see

The pretty follies that themselves commit ;
For if they could, Cupid himself would blush
To see me thus transformed to a boy.

  Lorenzo. Descend, for you must be my torch-
      bearer.   40

  Jessica. What, must I hold a candle to my shames?
They in themselves, good sooth, are too-too light.
Why, 't is an office of discovery, love,
And I should be obscur'd.

  Lorenzo.   So are you, sweet,
Even in the lovely garnish of a boy.
But come at once ;
For the close night doth play the runaway,
And we are stay'd for at Bassanio's feast.

  Jessica. I will make fast the doors, and gild myself
With some more ducats, and be with you straight.   50
                              [*Exit above.*

  Gratiano. Now, by my hood, a Gentile and no Jew.

  Lorenzo. Beshrew me but I love her heartily !
For she is wise, if I can judge of her ;
And fair she is, if that mine eyes be true ;
And true she is, as she hath prov'd herself ;
And therefore, like herself, wise, fair, and true,
Shall she be placed in my constant soul. —

Enter JESSICA, *below*

What, art thou come ? — On, gentlemen ; away !
Our masquing mates by this time for us stay.
                    [*Exit with Jessica and Salarino.*

Enter ANTONIO

Antonio. Who's there?   60
Gratiano. Signior Antonio!
Antonio. Fie, fie, Gratiano! where are all the rest?
'T is nine o'clock; our friends all stay for you.
No masque to-night: the wind is come about;
Bassanio presently will go aboard.
I have sent twenty out to seek for you.
Gratiano. I am glad on 't; I desire no more delight
Than to be under sail and gone to-night.   [*Exeunt.*

SCENE VII. *Belmont. A Room in Portia's House*

Flourish of cornets.   Enter PORTIA, *with the* PRINCE OF
MOROCCO, *and their trains*

Portia. Go, draw aside the curtains, and discover
The several caskets to this noble prince. —
Now make your choice.
Morocco. The first, of gold, who this inscription bears,
'*Who chooseth me shall gain what many men desire.*'
The second, silver, which this promise carries,
'*Who chooseth me shall get as much as he deserves.*'
This third, dull lead, with warning all as blunt,
'*Who chooseth me must give and hazard all he hath.*'
How shall I know if I do choose the right?   10
Portia. The one of them contains my picture, prince;
If you choose that, then I am yours withal.
Morocco. Some god direct my judgment! Let me see;

I will survey the inscriptions back again.
What says this leaden casket?
'*Who chooseth me must give and hazard all he hath.*'
Must give — for what? For lead? Hazard for lead?
This casket threatens. Men that hazard all
Do it in hope of fair advantages.
A golden mind stoops not to shows of dross; 20
I 'll then nor give nor hazard aught for lead.
What says the silver with her virgin hue?
'*Who chooseth me shall get as much as he deserves.*'
As much as he deserves? Pause there, Morocco,
And weigh thy value with an even hand.
If thou be'st rated by thy estimation,
Thou dost deserve enough; and yet enough
May not extend so far as to the lady;
And yet to be afeard of my deserving
Were but a weak disabling of myself. 30
As much as I deserve? Why, that 's the lady:
I do in birth deserve her, and in fortunes,
In graces and in qualities of breeding;
But more than these, in love I do deserve.
What if I stray'd no further, but chose here? —
Let 's see once more this saying grav'd in gold:
'*Who chooseth me shall gain what many men desire.*'
Why, that 's the lady: all the world desires her;
From the four corners of the earth they come,
To kiss this shrine, this mortal-breathing saint. 40
The Hyrcanian deserts and the vasty wilds
Of wide Arabia are as throughfares now

For princes to come view fair Portia.
The watery kingdom, whose ambitious head
Spets in the face of heaven, is no bar
To stop the foreign spirits, but they come,
As o'er a brook, to see fair Portia.
One of these three contains her heavenly picture.
Is 't like that lead contains her? 'T were damnation
To think so base a thought; it were too gross   50
To rib her cerecloth in the obscure grave.
Or shall I think in silver she 's immur'd,
Being ten times undervalued to tried gold?
O sinful thought! Never so rich a gem
Was set in worse than gold. They have in England
A coin that bears the figure of an angel
Stamped in gold, but that 's insculp'd upon;
But here an angel in a golden bed
Lies all within. — Deliver me the key;
Here do I choose, and thrive I as I may!   60
    Portia. There, take it, prince; and if my form lie
       there,
Then I am yours.   [*He unlocks the golden casket.*
    Morocco.   O hell! what have we here?
A carrion death, within whose empty eye
There is a written scroll! I 'll read the writing.
        'All that glisters is not gold;
        Often have you heard that told.
        Many a man his life hath sold,
        But my outside to behold;
        Gilded tombs do worms infold.

> *Had you been as wise as bold,*   70
> *Young in limbs, in judgment old,*
> *Your answer had not been inscroll'd:*
> *Fare you well; your suit is cold.'*
>   Cold, indeed, and labour lost;
>   Then, farewell, heat, and welcome, frost!
> Portia, adieu!   I have too griev'd a heart
> To take a tedious leave; thus losers part.

> *[Exit with his train.*

Portia. A gentle riddance. — Draw the curtains; go.
Let all of his complexion choose me so.

> *[Exeunt.   Flourish of cornets.*

SCENE VIII.   *Venice.   A Street*

Enter SALARINO *and* SALANIO

Salarino. Why, man, I saw Bassanio under sail;
With him is Gratiano gone along,
And in their ship I am sure Lorenzo is not.

Salanio. The villain Jew with outcries rais'd the duke,
Who went with him to search Bassanio's ship.

Salarino. He came too late, the ship was under sail;
But there the duke was given to understand
That in a gondola were seen together
Lorenzo and his amorous Jessica.
Besides, Antonio certified the duke   10
They were not with Bassanio in his ship.

Salanio. I never heard a passion so confus'd,
So strange, outrageous, and so variable,

As the dog Jew did utter in the streets :
' My daughter !   O my ducats !   O my daughter !
Fled with a Christian !   O my Christian ducats !
Justice ! the law ! my ducats, and my daughter !
A sealed bag, two sealed bags of ducats,
Of double ducats, stolen from me by my daughter !
And jewels, two stones, two rich and precious stones, 20
Stolen by my daughter !   Justice ! find the girl ;
She hath the stones upon her, and the ducats.'
 Salarino. Why, all the boys in Venice follow him,
Crying, his stones, his daughter, and his ducats.
 Salanio. Let good Antonio look he keep his day,
Or he shall pay for this.
 Salarino.   Marry, well remember'd.
I reason'd with a Frenchman yesterday,
Who told me, in the narrow seas that part
The French and English, there miscarried
A vessel of our country richly fraught. 30
I thought upon Antonio when he told me,
And wish'd in silence that it were not his.
 Salanio. You were best to tell Antonio what you hear ;
Yet do not suddenly, for it may grieve him.
 Salarino. A kinder gentleman treads not the earth.
I saw Bassanio and Antonio part.
Bassanio told him he would make some speed
Of his return ; he answer'd, ' Do not so ;
Slubber not business for my sake, Bassanio,
But stay the very riping of the time ; 40
And for the Jew's bond which he hath of me,

Let it not enter in your mind of love.
Be merry, and employ your chiefest thoughts
To courtship and such fair ostents of love
As shall conveniently become you there.'
And even there, his eye being big with tears,
Turning his face, he put his hand behind him,
And with affection wondrous sensible
He wrung Bassanio's hand; and so they parted.

    Salanio. I think he only loves the world for him. 50
I pray thee, let us go and find him out,
And quicken his embraced heaviness
With some delight or other.

    Salarino.   Do we so.   *[Exeunt.*

SCENE IX. *Belmont. A Room in Portia's House*

Enter NERISSA *with a* Servitor

    Nerissa. Quick, quick, I pray thee; draw the curtain
        straight.
The Prince of Arragon hath ta'en his oath,
And comes to his election presently.

Flourish of cornets. Enter the PRINCE OF ARRAGON,
PORTIA, *and their trains*

    Portia. Behold, there stand the caskets, noble prince.
If you choose that wherein I am contain'd,
Straight shall our nuptial rites be solemniz'd;
But if you fail, without more speech, my lord,
You must be gone from hence immediately.

Arragon. I am enjoin'd by oath to observe three
        things :
First, never to unfold to any one   10
Which casket 't was I chose ; next, if I fail
Of the right casket, never in my life
To woo a maid in way of marriage ;
Lastly, if I do fail in fortune of my choice,
Immediately to leave you and be gone.
    Portia. To these injunctions every one doth swear
That comes to hazard for my worthless self.
    Arragon. And so have I address'd me.   Fortune now
To my heart's hope ! — Gold, silver, and base lead.
' *Who chooseth me must give and hazard all he hath.*'   20
You shall look fairer ere I give or hazard.
What says the golden chest ? ha ! let me see :
' *Who chooseth me shall gain what many men desire.*'
What many men desire ! that many may be meant
By the fool multitude that choose by show,
Not learning more than the fond eye doth teach ;
Which pries not to the interior, but, like the martlet,
Builds in the weather, on the outward wall,
Even in the force and road of casualty.
I will not choose what many men desire,   30
Because I will not jump with common spirits
And rank me with the barbarous multitudes.
Why, then to thee, thou silver treasure-house ;
Tell me once more what title thou dost bear :
' *Who chooseth me shall get as much as he deserves :*'
And well said too ; for who shall go about

To cozen fortune and be honourable
Without the stamp of merit ?   Let none presume
To wear an undeserved dignity.
O, that estates, degrees, and offices   40
Were not deriv'd corruptly, and that clear honour
Were purchas'd by the merit of the wearer !
How many then should cover that stand bare !
How many be commanded that command !
How much low peasantry would then be glean'd
From the true seed of honour ; and how much honour
Pick'd from the chaff and ruin of the times,
To be new-varnish'd !   Well, but to my choice :
'*Who chooseth me shall get as much as he deserves.*'
I will assume desert. — Give me a key for this,   50
And instantly unlock my fortunes here.

> > > > > > *[He opens the silver casket.*

   Portia. Too long a pause for that which you find
      there.
   Arragon. What's here ? the portrait of a blinking
      idiot,
Presenting me a schedule !   I will read it.
How much unlike art thou to Portia !
How much unlike my hopes and my deservings !
'*Who chooseth me shall have as much as he deserves.*'
Did I deserve no more than a fool's head ?
Is that my prize ? are my deserts no better ?
   Portia. To offend and judge are distinct offices,   60
And of opposed natures.
   Arragon.   What is here ?

     ' *The fire seven times tried this;*
     Seven times tried that judgment is,
     That did never choose amiss.
     Some there be that shadows kiss;
     Such have but a shadow's bliss.
     There be fools alive, I wis,
     Silver'd o'er; and so was this.
     Take what wife you will to bed,
     I will ever be your head.   70
     So be gone; you are sped.'
Still more fool I shall appear
By the time I linger here;
With one fool's head I came to woo,
But I go away with two. —
Sweet, adieu! I 'll keep my oath,
Patiently to bear my wroth.
               [*Exeunt Arragon and train.*
  Portia. Thus hath the candle sing'd the moth.
O, these deliberate fools! when they do choose,
They have the wisdom by their wit to lose.   80
  Nerissa. The ancient saying is no heresy, —
Hanging and wiving goes by destiny.
  Portia. Come, draw the curtain, Nerissa.

Enter a Servant

  Servant. Where is my lady?
  Portia.   Here; what would my lord?
  Servant. Madam, there is alighted at your gate
A young Venetian, one that comes before

To signify the approaching of his lord,
From whom he bringeth sensible regreets;
To wit, besides commends and courteous breath,
Gifts of rich value.   Yet I have not seen   90
So likely an ambassador of love;
A day in April never came so sweet,
To show how costly summer was at hand,
As this fore-spurrer comes before his lord.
  Portia. No more, I pray thee; I am half afeard
Thou wilt say anon he is some kin to thee,
Thou spend'st such high-day wit in praising him. —
Come, come, Nerissa; for I long to see
Quick Cupid's post that comes so mannerly.
  Nerissa. Bassanio, lord Love, if thy will it be !   100
                                  [*Exeunt.*

RIALTO BRIDGE

ACT III

SCENE I. *Venice. A Street*

Enter SALANIO *and* SALARINO

Salanio. Now, what news on the Rialto?

Salarino. Why, yet it lives there unchecked that
Antonio hath a ship of rich lading wracked on the
narrow seas — the Goodwins I think they call the
place; a very dangerous flat and fatal, where the car-
casses of many a tall ship lie buried, as they say, if
my gossip Report be an honest woman of her word.

Salanio. I would she were as lying a gossip in
that as ever knapped ginger, or made her neigh-

bours believe she wept for the death of a third hus- 10
band.   But it is true, without any slips of prolixity
or crossing the plain highway of talk, that the good
Antonio, the honest Antonio, — O that I had a title
good enough to keep his name company ! —

Salarino. Come, the full stop.

Salanio. Ha ! what sayest thou ? — Why, the end
is, he hath lost a ship.

Salarino. I would it might prove the end of his
losses !

Salanio. Let me say amen betimes, lest the devil 20
cross my prayer ; for here he comes in the likeness
of a Jew. —

Enter SHYLOCK

How now, Shylock ? what news among the merchants ?

Shylock. You knew, none so well, none so well as
you, of my daughter's flight.

Salarino. That 's certain ; I, for my part, knew the
tailor that made the wings she flew withal.

Salanio. And Shylock, for his own part, knew the
bird was fledged ; and then it is the complexion of
them all to leave the dam.   30

Shylock. My own flesh and blood to rebel !

Salarino. There is more difference between thy
flesh and hers than between jet and ivory ; more
between your bloods than there is between red wine
and Rhenish.   But tell us, do you hear whether
Antonio have had any loss at sea or no ?

Shylock. There I have another bad match : a bank-

rupt, a prodigal, who dare scarce show his head on
the Rialto ; a beggar, that was used to come so smug
upon the mart.   Let him look to his bond : he was 40
wont to call me usurer ; let him look to his bond :
he was wont to lend money for a Christian courtesy ;
let him look to his bond.

Salarino.   Why, I am sure, if he forfeit, thou wilt
not take his flesh ; what 's that good for ?

Shylock.   To bait fish withal ; if it will feed nothing else, it will feed my revenge.   He hath disgraced
me and hindered me half a million, laughed at my
losses, mocked at my gains, scorned my nation,
thwarted my bargains, cooled my friends, heated 50
mine enemies ; and what 's his reason ?   I am a Jew.
Hath not a Jew eyes ? hath not a Jew hands, organs,
dimensions, senses, affections, passions ? fed with the
same food, hurt with the same weapons, subject to
the same diseases, healed by the same means, warmed
and cooled by the same winter and summer, as a
Christian is ?   If you prick us, do we not bleed ? if
you tickle us, do we not laugh ? if you poison us,
do we not die ? and if you wrong us, shall we not
revenge ?   If we are like you in the rest, we will 60
resemble you in that.   If a Jew wrong a Christian,
what is his humility?   Revenge.   If a Christian
wrong a Jew, what should his sufferance be, by
Christian example ?   Why, revenge.   The villany
you teach me, I will execute ; and it shall go hard
but I will better the instruction.

Enter a Servant

Servant. Gentlemen, my master Antonio is at his house, and desires to speak with you both.

Salarino. We have been up and down to seek him.

Enter TUBAL

Salanio. Here comes another of the tribe ; a third 70 cannot be matched, unless the devil himself turn Jew.   [*Exeunt Salanio, Salarino, and Servant.*

Shylock. How now, Tubal ? what news from Genoa ? hast thou found my daughter ?

Tubal. I often came where I did hear of her, but cannot find her.

Shylock. Why, there, there, there, there ! a diamond gone, cost me two thousand ducats in Frankfort ! The curse never fell upon our nation till now ; I never felt it till now ; two thousand ducats in that, 80 and other precious, precious jewels. I would my daughter were dead at my foot, and the jewels in her ear ! Would she were hearsed at my foot, and the ducats in her coffin ! No news of them ?— Why, so ; and I know not how much is spent in the search. Why, thou loss upon loss ! the thief gone with so much, and so much to find the thief ; and no satisfaction, no revenge ; nor no ill luck stirring but what lights o' my shoulders ; no sighs but o' my breathing, no tears but o' my shedding.   90

Tubal. Yes, other men have ill luck too. Antonio, as I heard in Genoa, —

Shylock. What, what, what? ill luck, ill luck?

Tubal. Hath an argosy cast away, coming from Tripolis.

Shylock. I thank God! I thank God! Is it true? is it true?

Tubal. I spoke with some of the sailors that escaped the wrack.

Shylock. I thank thee, good Tubal! — Good news, good news! ha, ha! — Where? in Genoa? 100

Tubal. Your daughter spent in Genoa, as I heard, in one night fourscore ducats.

Shylock. Thou stick'st a dagger in me. I shall never see my gold again. Fourscore ducats at a sitting! fourscore ducats!

Tubal. There came divers of Antonio's creditors in my company to Venice, that swear he cannot choose but break.

Shylock. I am very glad of it. I 'll plague him; I 'll torture him. I am glad of it. 110

Tubal. One of them showed me a ring that he had of your daughter for a monkey.

Shylock. Out upon her! Thou torturest me, Tubal. It was my turquoise; I had it of Leah when I was a bachelor. I would not have given it for a wilderness of monkeys.

Tubal. But Antonio is certainly undone.

Shylock. Nay, that 's true, that 's very true. Go, Tubal, fee me an officer; bespeak him a fortnight before. I will have the heart of him, if he forfeit; 120

for, were he out of Venice, I can make what merchandise I will. Go, go, Tubal, and meet me at
our synagogue : go, good Tubal; at our synagogue,
Tubal. [*Exeunt.*

SCENE II. *Belmont. A Room in Portia's House*

Enter BASSANIO, PORTIA, GRATIANO, NERISSA, *and*
Attendants

Portia. I pray you, tarry : pause a day or two
Before you hazard, for, in choosing wrong,
I lose your company ; therefore forbear a while.
There 's something tells me, but it is not love,
I would not lose you ; and you know yourself,
Hate counsels not in such a quality.
But lest you should not understand me well, —
And yet a maiden hath no tongue but thought, —
I would detain you here some month or two
Before you venture for me. I could teach you   10
How to choose right, but then I am forsworn ;
So will I never be. So may you miss me ;
But if you do, you 'll make me wish a sin,
That I had been forsworn. Beshrew your eyes,
They have o'erlook'd me and divided me ;
One half of me is yours, the other half yours, —
Mine own, I would say ; but if mine, then yours,
And so all yours. O, these naughty times
Put bars between the owners and their rights !
And so, though yours, not yours. Prove it so,   20

Let fortune go to hell for it, not I.
I speak too long; but 't is to peize the time,
To eke it, and to draw it out in length,
To stay you from election.

    Bassanio.   Let me choose;
For as I am, I live upon the rack.

    Portia. Upon the rack, Bassanio! then confess
What treason there is mingled with your love.

    Bassanio. None but that ugly treason of mistrust
Which makes me fear the enjoying of my love.
There may as well be amity and life   *(league)*   30
'Tween snow and fire as treason and my love.

    Portia. Ay, but I fear you speak upon the rack,
Where men enforced do speak any thing.

    Bassanio. Promise me life, and I'll confess the truth.

    Portia. Well then, confess and live.

    Bassanio.   Confess and love
Had been the very sum of my confession.
O happy torment, when my torturer
Doth teach me answers for deliverance!
But let me to my fortune and the caskets.

    Portia. Away, then! I am lock'd in one of them; 40
If you do love me, you will find me out. —
Nerissa and the rest, stand all aloof. —
Let music sound while he doth make his choice;
Then, if he lose, he makes a swan-like end,
Fading in music: that the comparison
May stand more proper, my eye shall be the stream
And watery death-bed for him. He may win;

And what is music then? Then music is
Even as the flourish when true subjects bow
To a new-crowned monarch; such it is   50
As are those dulcet sounds in break of day
That creep into the dreaming bridegroom's ear
And summon him to marriage. Now he goes,
With no less presence, but with much more love,
Than young Alcides, when he did redeem
The virgin tribute paid by howling Troy
To the sea-monster. I stand for sacrifice;
The rest aloof are the Dardanian wives,
With bleared visages, come forth to view
The issue of the exploit. Go, Hercules!   60
Live thou, I live. — With much more dismay
I view the fight than thou that mak'st the fray.

A Song, whilst BASSANIO *comments on the caskets to himself.*

> *Tell me where is fancy bred,*
> *Or in the heart or in the head?*
> *How begot, how nourished?*
> *Reply, reply.*

> *It is engender'd in the eyes,*
> *With gazing fed; and fancy dies*
> *In the cradle where it lies.*
> > *Let us all ring fancy's knell;*   70
> > *I'll begin it, — Ding, dong, bell.*
> All. *Ding, dong, bell.*

Bassanio. So may the outward shows be least them-
        selves ;
The world is still deceiv'd with ornament.
In law, what plea so tainted and corrupt
But, being season'd with a gracious voice,
Obscures the show of evil ?   In religion,
What damned error, but some sober brow
Will bless it and approve it with a text,
Hiding the grossness with fair ornament?   80
There is no vice so simple but assumes
Some mark of virtue on his outward parts.
How many cowards, whose hearts are all as false
As stairs of sand, wear yet upon their chins
The beards of Hercules and frowning Mars,
Who, inward search'd, have livers white as milk ;
And these assume but valour's excrement
To render them redoubted !   Look on beauty,
And you shall see 't is purchas'd by the weight,
Which therein works a miracle in nature,   90
Making them lightest that wear most of it.
So are those crisped snaky golden locks,
Which make such wanton gambols with the wind,
Upon supposed fairness, often known
To be the dowry of a second head,
The skull that bred them in the sepulchre.
Thus ornament is but the guiled shore
To a most dangerous sea, the beauteous scarf
Veiling an Indian beauty, — in a word,
The seeming truth which cunning times put on   100

To entrap the wisest. Therefore, thou gaudy gold,
Hard food for Midas, I will none of thee;
Nor none of thee, thou pale and common drudge
'Tween man and man; but thou, thou meagre lead,
Which rather threatenest than dost promise aught,
Thy plainness moves me more than eloquence,
And here choose I. Joy be the consequence!

Portia. [*Aside*] How all the other passions fleet to air,
As doubtful thoughts, and rash-embrac'd despair,
And shuddering fear, and green-eyed jealousy! 110
O love! be moderate; allay thy ecstasy;
In measure rain thy joy; scant this excess.
I feel too much thy blessing; make it less,
For fear I surfeit.

Bassanio. What find I here?

[*Opening the leaden casket.*

Fair Portia's counterfeit! What demigod
Hath come so near creation? Move these eyes?
Or whether, riding on the balls of mine
Seem they in motion? Here are sever'd lips,
Parted with sugar breath; so sweet a bar
Should sunder such sweet friends. Here in her hairs 120
The painter plays the spider, and hath woven
A golden mesh to entrap the hearts of men
Faster than gnats in cobwebs. But her eyes!—
How could he see to do them? having made one,
Methinks it should have power to steal both his
And leave itself unfurnish'd. Yet look, how far
The substance of my praise doth wrong this shadow

In underprizing it, so far this shadow
Doth limp behind the substance. — Here's the scroll,
The continent and summary of my fortune.   130

> ' *You that choose not by the view*
> *Chance as fair and choose as true !*
> *Since this fortune falls to you,*
> *Be content and seek no new.*
> *If you be well pleas'd with this,*
> *And hold your fortune for your bliss,*
> *Turn you where your lady is,*
> *And claim her with a loving kiss.'*

A gentle scroll. — Fair lady, by your leave ;
I come by note, to give and to receive.   [*Kissing her.*
Like one of two contending in a prize,   141
That thinks he hath done well in people's eyes,
Hearing applause and universal shout,
Giddy in spirit, still gazing in a doubt
Whether those peals of praise be his or no ;
So, thrice-fair lady, stand I, even so,
As doubtful whether what I see be true,
Until confirm'd, sign'd, ratified by you.

Portia.   You see me, Lord Bassanio, where I stand,
Such as I am.   Though for myself alone   150
I would not be ambitious in my wish,
To wish myself much better, yet for you
I would be trebled twenty times myself,
A thousand times more fair, ten thousand times more
    rich,

That only to stand high in your account,
I might in virtues, beauties, livings, friends,
Exceed account.   But the full sum of me
Is sum of nothing; which, to term in gross,
Is an unlesson'd girl, unschool'd, unpractis'd:
Happy in this, she is not yet so old   160
But she may learn; happier than this,
She is not bred so dull but she can learn;
Happiest of all in that her gentle spirit
Commits itself to yours to be directed,
As from her lord, her governor, her king.
Myself and what is mine to you and yours
Is now converted.   But now I was the lord
Of this fair mansion, master of my servants,
Queen o'er myself; and even now, but now,
This house, these servants, and this same myself   170
Are yours, my lord.   I give them with this ring,
Which when you part from, lose, or give away,
Let it presage the ruin of your love,
And be my vantage to exclaim on you.
 Bassanio. Madam, you have bereft me of all words,
Only my blood speaks to you in my veins;
And there is such confusion in my powers
As, after some oration fairly spoke
By a beloved prince, there doth appear
Among the buzzing pleased multitude,   180
Where every something, being blent together,
Turns to a wild of nothing, save of joy,
Express'd and not express'd.   But when this ring

Parts from this finger, then parts life from hence ;
O, then be bold to say Bassanio's dead !

Nerissa. My lord and lady, it is now our time,
That have stood by and seen our wishes prosper,
To cry, good joy. Good joy, my lord and lady !

Gratiano. My lord Bassanio and my gentle lady,
I wish you all the joy that you can wish,   190
For I am sure you can wish none from me ;
And when your honours mean to solemnize
The bargain of your faith, I do beseech you,
Even at that time I may be married too.

Bassanio. With all my heart, so thou canst get a wife.

Gratiano. I thank your lordship, you have got me one.
My eyes, my lord, can look as swift as yours.
You saw the mistress, I beheld the maid ;
You lov'd, I lov'd ; for intermission
No more pertains to me, my lord, than you.   200
Your fortune stood upon the caskets there,
And so did mine too, as the matter falls ;
For wooing here until I sweat again,
And swearing till my very roof was dry
With oaths of love, at last, if promise last,
I got a promise of this fair one here
To have her love, provided that your fortune
Achiev'd her mistress.

Portia.   Is this true, Nerissa ?

Nerissa. Madam, it is, so you stand pleas'd withal.

Bassanio. And do you, Gratiano, mean good faith ? 210

Gratiano. Yes, faith, my lord.

Bassanio. Our feast shall be much honour'd in your
marriage.

Gratiano. But who comes here? Lorenzo and his
infidel?

What! and my old Venetian friend, Salerio?

Enter LORENZO, JESSICA, *and* SALERIO, *a messenger
from Venice*

Bassanio. Lorenzo and Salerio, welcome hither;
If that the youth of my new interest here
Have power to bid you welcome. — By your leave,
I bid my very friends and countrymen,
Sweet Portia, welcome.

Portia.　　　　　So do I, my lord;
They are entirely welcome.　　　　　　　　　220

Lorenzo. I thank your honour. — For my part, my lord,
My purpose was not to have seen you here;
But meeting with Salerio by the way,
He did entreat me, past all saying nay,
To come with him along.

Salerio.　　　　　I did, my lord,
And I have reason for it. Signior Antonio
Commends him to you.　　　*[Gives Bassanio a letter.*

Bassanio.　　　　　Ere I ope his letter,
I pray you, tell me how my good friend doth.

Salerio. Not sick, my lord, unless it be in mind,
Nor well, unless in mind; his letter there　　230
Will show you his estate.

MER. OF VEN. — 7

Gratiano. Nerissa, cheer yon stranger; bid her wel-
come. —
Your hand, Salerio; what's the news from Venice?
How doth that royal merchant, good Antonio?
I know he will be glad of our success;
We are the Jasons, we have won the fleece.

    Salerio. I would you had won the fleece that he hath
lost!

    Portia. There are some shrewd contents in yon same
paper,
That steals the colour from Bassanio's cheek:
Some dear friend dead; else nothing in the world   240
Could turn so much the constitution
Of any constant man. What, worse and worse? —
With leave, Bassanio; I am half yourself,
And I must freely have the half of any thing
That this same paper brings you.

    Bassanio.   O sweet Portia,
Here are a few of the unpleasant'st words
That ever blotted paper! Gentle lady,
When I did first impart my love to you,
I freely told you, all the wealth I had
Ran in my veins — I was a gentleman.   250
And then I told you true; and yet, dear lady,
Rating myself at nothing, you shall see
How much I was a braggart. When I told you
My state was nothing, I should then have told you
That I was worse than nothing; for indeed
I have engag'd myself to a dear friend,

Engag'd my friend to his mere enemy,
To feed my means.   Here is a letter, lady;
The paper as the body of my friend,
And every word in it a gaping wound,   260
Issuing life-blood. — But is it true, Salerio?
Have all his ventures fail'd?   What, not one hit?
From Tripolis, from Mexico, and England,
From Lisbon, Barbary, and India,
And not one vessel scape the dreadful touch
Of merchant-marring rocks?

 Salerio.   Not one, my lord.
Besides, it should appear that if he had
The present money to discharge the Jew,
He would not take it.   Never did I know
A creature that did bear the shape of man,   270
So keen and greedy to confound a man.
He plies the duke at morning and at night,
And doth impeach the freedom of the state,
If they deny him justice.   Twenty merchants,
The duke himself, and the magnificoes
Of greatest port, have all persuaded with him;
But none can drive him from the envious plea
Of forfeiture, of justice, and his bond.

 Jessica. When I was with him I have heard him
   swear
To Tubal and to Chus, his countrymen,   280
That he would rather have Antonio's flesh
Than twenty times the value of the sum
That he did owe him; and I know, my lord,

If law, authority, and power deny not,
It will go hard with poor Antonio.

   Portia. Is it your dear friend that is thus in trouble?

   Bassanio. The dearest friend to me, the kindest man,
The best-condition'd and unwearied spirit
In doing courtesies; and one in whom
The ancient Roman honour more appears   290
Than any that draws breath in Italy.

   Portia. What sum owes he the Jew?

   Bassanio. For me, three thousand ducats.

   Portia.   What, no more?
Pay him six thousand, and deface the bond;
Double six thousand, and then treble that,
Before a friend of this description
Shall lose a hair through Bassanio's fault.
First go with me to church and call me wife,
And then away to Venice to your friend;
For never shall you lie by Portia's side   300
With an unquiet soul.   You shall have gold
To pay the petty debt twenty times over;
When it is paid, bring your true friend along.
My maid Nerissa and myself, mean time,
Will live as maids and widows.   Come, away!
For you shall hence upon your wedding-day.
Bid your friends welcome, show a merry cheer;
Since you are dear bought, I will love you dear. —
But let me hear the letter of your friend.

   Bassanio. [Reads] '*Sweet Bassanio, my ships have* 310

all miscarried, my creditors grow cruel, my estate is very
low, my bond to the Jew is forfeit; and since, in paying
it, it is impossible I should live, all debts are cleared
between you and I, if I might see you at my death.
Notwithstanding, use your pleasure; if your love do
not persuade you to come, let not my letter.'

   Portia. O love, dispatch all business, and be gone!
   Bassanio. Since I have your good leave to go away,
   I will make haste; but, till I come again,
No bed shall e'er be guilty of my stay,   320
   Nor rest be interposer 'twixt us twain.   [*Exeunt.*

SCENE III.   *Venice.   A Street*

Enter SHYLOCK, SALARINO, ANTONIO, *and* Gaoler

   Shylock. Gaoler, look to him; tell not me of
      mercy. —
This is the fool that lends out money gratis. —
Gaoler, look to him.
   Antonio.   Hear me yet, good Shylock.
   Shylock. I 'll have my bond; speak not against my
      bond.
I have sworn an oath that I will have my bond.
Thou call'dst me dog before thou hadst a cause;
But, since I am a dog, beware my fangs.
The duke shall grant me justice. — I do wonder,
Thou naughty gaoler, that thou art so fond
To come abroad with him at his request.   10

Antonio. I pray thee, hear me speak.

Shylock. I 'll have my bond; I will not hear thee
    speak.

I 'll have my bond; and therefore speak no more.
I 'll not be made a soft and dull-eyed fool,
To shake the head, relent, and sigh, and yield
To Christian intercessors.   Follow not;
I 'll have no speaking; I will have my bond.   [*Exit.*

Salarino. It is the most impenetrable cur
That ever kept with men.

Antonio.   Let him alone;
I 'll follow him no more with bootless prayers.   20
He seeks my life; his reason well I know.
I oft deliver'd from his forfeitures
Many that have at times made moan to me;
Therefore he hates me.

Salarino.   I am sure the duke
Will never grant this forfeiture to hold.

Antonio. The duke cannot deny the course of law;
For the commodity that strangers have
With us in Venice, if it be denied,
Will much impeach the justice of the state,
Since that the trade and profit of the city   30
Consisteth of all nations.   Therefore go;
These griefs and losses have so bated me
That I shall hardly spare a pound of flesh
To-morrow to my bloody creditor. —
Well, gaoler, on. — Pray God, Bassanio come
To see me pay his debt, and then I care not! [*Exeunt.*

SCENE IV. *Belmont. A Room in Portia's House*

Enter PORTIA, NERISSA, LORENZO, JESSICA, *and* BALTHASAR

Lorenzo. Madam, although I speak it in your presence,
You have a noble and a true conceit
Of godlike amity, which appears most strongly
In bearing thus the absence of your lord.
But if you knew to whom you show this honour,
How true a gentleman you send relief,
How dear a lover of my lord your husband,
I know you would be prouder of the work
Than customary bounty can enforce you.

Portia. I never did repent for doing good, 10
Nor shall not now; for in companions
That do converse and waste the time together,
Whose souls do bear an equal yoke of love,
There must be needs a like proportion
Of lineaments, of manners, and of spirit;
Which makes me think that this Antonio,
Being the bosom lover of my lord,
Must needs be like my lord. If it be so,
How little is the cost I have bestow'd
In purchasing the semblance of my soul 20
From out the state of hellish cruelty!
This comes too near the praising of myself,
Therefore no more of it; hear other things.

Lorenzo, I commit into your hands
The husbandry and manage of my house
Until my lord's return; for mine own part,
I have toward heaven breath'd a secret vow
To live in prayer and contemplation,
Only attended by Nerissa here,
Until her husband and my lord's return.   30
There is a monastery two miles off,
And there will we abide.   I do desire you
Not to deny this imposition,
The which my love and some necessity
Now lays upon you.
    Lorenzo.   Madam, with all my heart;
I shall obey you in all fair commands.
    Portia. My people do already know my mind,
And will acknowledge you and Jessica
In place of Lord Bassanio and myself.
So fare you well till we shall meet again.   40
    Lorenzo. Fair thoughts and happy hours attend on
       you!
    Jessica. I wish your ladyship all heart's content.
    Portia. I thank you for your wish, and am well pleas'd
To wish it back on you; fare you well, Jessica.—
                    [*Exeunt Jessica and Lorenzo.*
Now, Balthasar,
As I have ever found thee honest-true,
So let me find thee still.   Take this same letter,
And use thou all the endeavour of a man
In speed to Padua.   See thou render this

Into my cousin's hand, Doctor Bellario ; 50
And, look, what notes and garments he doth give thee,
Bring them, I pray thee, with imagin'd speed
Unto the tranect, to the common ferry
Which trades to Venice. Waste no time in words,
But get thee gone ; I shall be there before thee.

   Balthasar. Madam, I go with all convenient speed.

                                      [Exit.

   Portia. Come on, Nerissa ; I have work in hand
That you yet know not of. We 'll see our husbands
Before they think of us.

   Nerissa.   Shall they see us ?

   Portia. They shall, Nerissa, but in such a habit 60
That they shall think we are accomplished
With that we lack. I 'll hold thee any wager,
When we are both accoutred like young men,
I 'll prove the prettier fellow of the two,
And wear my dagger with the braver grace,
And speak between the change of man and boy
With a reed voice, and turn two mincing steps
Into a manly stride, and speak of frays
Like a fine bragging youth ; and tell quaint lies,
How honourable ladies sought my love, 70
Which I denying, they fell sick and died,
I could not do withal ; then I 'll repent,
And wish, for all that, that I had not kill'd them.
And twenty of these puny lies I'll tell,
That men shall swear I have discontinued school
Above a twelvemonth. I have within my mind

A thousand raw tricks of these bragging Jacks
Which I will practise.
But come, I 'll tell thee all my whole device
When I am in my coach, which stays for us   80
At the park gate; and therefore haste away,
For we must measure twenty miles to-day.   [*Exeunt.*

SCENE V.   *The Same.   A Garden*

Enter LAUNCELOT *and* JESSICA

Launcelot. Yes, truly; for, look you, the sins of the
father are to be laid upon the children; therefore, I
promise you, I fear you. I was always plain with
you, and so now I speak my agitation of the matter;
therefore be of good cheer, for truly I think you are
damned. There is but one hope in it that can do
you any good.

Jessica. And what hope is that, I pray thee?

Launcelot. Marry, you may partly hope that you
are not the Jew's daughter.   10

Jessica. So the sins of my mother should be visited
upon me.

Launcelot. Truly then I fear you are damned both
by father and mother; thus when I shun Scylla, your
father, I fall into Charybdis, your mother. Well,
you are gone both ways.

Jessica. I shall be saved by my husband; he hath
made me a Christian.

Launcelot. Truly, the more to blame he; we were Christians enow before, e'en as many as could well 20 live, one by another. This making of Christians will raise the price of hogs; if we grow all to be pork-eaters, we shall not shortly have a rasher on the coals for money.

Enter LORENZO

Jessica. I 'll tell my husband, Launcelot, what you say; here he comes.

Lorenzo. I shall grow jealous of you shortly, Launcelot.

Jessica. Nay, you need not fear us, Lorenzo; Launcelot and I are out. He tells me flatly, there 30 is no mercy for me in heaven, because I am a Jew's daughter; and he says you are no good member of the commonwealth, for in converting Jews to Christians you raise the price of pork.

Lorenzo. I think the best grace of wit will shortly turn into silence, and discourse grow commendable in none only but parrots. — Go in, sirrah; bid them prepare for dinner.

Launcelot. That is done, sir; they have all stomachs.   40

Lorenzo. Goodly Lord, what a wit-snapper are you! then bid them prepare dinner.

Launcelot. That is done too, sir; only, cover is the word.

Lorenzo. Will you cover then, sir?

Launcelot. Not so, sir, neither; I know my duty.

Lorenzo. Yet more quarrelling with occasion!
Wilt thou show the whole wealth of thy wit in an
instant? I pray thee, understand a plain man in his
plain meaning: go to thy fellows; bid them cover 50
the table, serve in the meat, and we will come in to
dinner.

Launcelot. For the table, sir, it shall be served in;
for the meat, sir, it shall be covered; for your coming in to dinner, sir, why, let it be as humours and
conceits shall govern.   [*Exit.*

Lorenzo. O dear discretion, how his words are
            suited!
The fool hath planted in his memory
An army of good words; and I do know
A many fools that stand in better place,   60
Garnish'd like him, that for a tricksy word
Defy the matter. — How cheer'st thou, Jessica?
And now, good sweet, say thy opinion,
How dost thou like the lord Bassanio's wife?

Jessica. Past all expressing. It is very meet
The lord Bassanio live an upright life,
For, having such a blessing in his lady,
He finds the joys of heaven here on earth;
And if on earth he do not mean it, then
In reason he should never come to heaven.   70
Why, if two gods should play some heavenly match,
And on the wager lay two earthly women,
And Portia one, there must be something else

Pawn'd with the other, for the poor rude world
Hath not her fellow.

 Lorenzo.   Even such a husband
Hast thou of me as she is for a wife.

 Jessica. Nay, but ask my opinion too of that.

 Lorenzo. I will anon ; first, let us go to dinner.

 Jessica. Nay, let me praise you while I have a
  stomach.

 Lorenzo. No, pray thee, let it serve for table-talk ; 80
Then, howsoe'er thou speak'st, 'mong other things
I shall digest it.

 Jessica. Well, I 'll set you forth. [*Exeunt.*

ACT IV

Scene I. *Venice. A Court of Justice*

Enter the Duke, *the* Magnificoes, Antonio, Bassanio,
Gratiano, Salerio, *and others*

Duke. What, is Antonio here?

Antonio. Ready, so please your grace.

Duke. I am sorry for thee; thou art come to answer
A stony adversary, an inhuman wretch
Uncapable of pity, void and empty
From any dram of mercy.

Antonio.   I have heard
Your grace hath ta'en great pains to qualify
His rigorous course; but since he stands obdurate

And that no lawful means can carry me
Out of his envy's reach, I do oppose   10
My patience to his fury, and am arm'd
To suffer, with a quietness of spirit,
The very tyranny and rage of his.
 Duke. Go one, and call the Jew into the court.
 Salerio. He is ready at the door; he comes, my lord.

Enter SHYLOCK

 Duke. Make room, and let him stand before our
   face. —
Shylock, the world thinks, and I think so too,
That thou but lead'st this fashion of thy malice
To the last hour of act; and then 't is thought
Thou 'lt show thy mercy and remorse, more strange   20
Than is thy strange apparent cruelty;
And where thou now exact'st the penalty,
Which is a pound of this poor merchant's flesh,
Thou wilt not only loose the forfeiture,
But, touch'd with human gentleness and love,
Forgive a moiety of the principal;
Glancing an eye of pity on his losses,
That have of late so huddled on his back,
Enow to press a royal merchant down,
And pluck commiseration of his state   30
From brassy bosoms and rough hearts of flint,
From stubborn Turks and Tartars, never train'd
To offices of tender courtesy.
We all expect a gentle answer, Jew.

Shylock. I have possess'd your grace of what I pur-
        pose,
And by our holy Sabbath have I sworn
To have the due and forfeit of my bond.
If you deny it, let the danger light
Upon your charter and your city's freedom.
You 'll ask me why I rather choose to have   40
A weight of carrion flesh than to receive
Three thousand ducats.   I 'll not answer that;
But, say, it is my humour: is it answer'd?
What if my house be troubled with a rat,
And I be pleas'd to give ten thousand ducats
To have it ban'd?   What, are you answer'd yet?
Some men there are love not a gaping pig,
Some that are mad if they behold a cat;
Masters of passion sway it to the mood
Of what it likes or loathes.   Now, for your answer: 50
As there is no firm reason to be render'd
Why he cannot abide a gaping pig,
Why he a harmless necessary cat,
So can I give no reason, nor I will not,
More than a lodg'd hate and a certain loathing
I bear Antonio, that I follow thus
A losing suit against him.   Are you answer'd?
        Bassanio. This is no answer, thou unfeeling man,
To excuse the current of thy cruelty.
        Shylock. I am not bound to please thee with my
        answer.   60
        Bassanio. Do all men kill the things they do not love?

Shylock. Hates any man the thing he would not kill?
Bassanio. Every offence is not a hate at first.
Shylock. What, wouldst thou have a serpent sting thee
    twice?
Antonio. I pray you, think you question with the
    Jew.
You may as well go stand upon the beach,
And bid the main flood bate his usual height;
You may as well use question with the wolf
Why he hath made the ewe bleat for the lamb;
You may as well forbid the mountain pines   70
To wag their high tops and to make no noise,
When they are fretted with the gusts of heaven;
You may as well do any thing most hard,
As seek to soften that — than which what's harder? —
His Jewish heart.   Therefore, I do beseech you,
Make no more offers, use no farther means,
But with all brief and plain conveniency
Let me have judgment, and the Jew his will.
    Bassanio. For thy three thousand ducats here is six.
    Shylock. If every ducat in six thousand ducats   80
Were in six parts, and every part a ducat,
I would not draw them; I would have my bond.
    Duke. How shalt thou hope for mercy, rendering
    none?
    Shylock. What judgment shall I dread, doing no
    wrong?
You have among you many a purchas'd slave,
Which, like your asses and your dogs and mules,
MER. OF VEN. — 8

You use in abject and in slavish parts,
Because you bought them.   Shall I say to you,
Let them be free, marry them to your heirs?
Why sweat they under burthens? let their beds   90
Be made as soft as yours, and let their palates
Be season'd with such viands?   You will answer,
The slaves are ours. — So do I answer you:
The pound of flesh which I demand of him
Is dearly bought; 't is mine, and I will have it.
If you deny me, fie upon your law!
There is no force in the decrees of Venice.
I stand for judgment.   Answer; shall I have it?

    Duke. Upon my power I may dismiss this court
Unless Bellario, a learned doctor,   100
Whom I have sent for to determine this,
Come here to-day.

    Salerio.   My lord, here stays without
A messenger with letters from the doctor,
New come from Padua.

    Duke. Bring us the letters; call the messenger.

    Bassanio. Good cheer, Antonio! What, man, courage yet!
The Jew shall have my flesh, blood, bones, and all,
Ere thou shalt lose for me one drop of blood.

    Antonio. I am a tainted wether of the flock,
Meetest for death; the weakest kind of fruit   110
Drops earliest to the ground, and so let me.
You cannot better be employ'd, Bassanio,
Than to live still and write mine epitaph.

Enter NERISSA, *dressed like a lawyer's clerk*

Duke. Came you from Padua, from Bellario?

Nerissa. From both, my lord. Bellario greets your
grace. [*Presenting a letter.*

Bassanio. Why dost thou whet thy knife so earnestly?

Shylock. To cut the forfeiture from that bankrupt
there.

Gratiano. Not on thy sole, but on thy soul, harsh Jew,
Thou mak'st thy knife keen; but no metal can,
No, not the hangman's axe, bear half the keenness 120
Of thy sharp envy. Can no prayers pierce thee?

Shylock. No, none that thou hast wit enough to make.

Gratiano. O, be thou damn'd, inexorable dog!
And for thy life let justice be accus'd!
Thou almost mak'st me waver in my faith,
To hold opinion with Pythagoras,
That souls of animals infuse themselves
Into the trunks of men. Thy currish spirit
Govern'd a wolf, who, hang'd for human slaughter,
Even from the gallows did his fell soul fleet, 130
And, whilst thou lay'st in thy unhallow'd dam,
Infus'd itself in thee; for thy desires
Are wolvish, bloody, starv'd, and ravenous.

Shylock. Till thou canst rail the seal from off my bond
Thou but offend'st thy lungs to speak so loud.
Repair thy wit, good youth, or it will fall
To cureless ruin. — I stand here for law.

Duke. This letter from Bellario doth commend

A young and learned doctor to our court. —
Where is he?

   Nerissa.   He attendeth here hard by,   14⌀
To know your answer, whether you 'll admit him.

   Duke. With all my heart. — Some three or four of
       you
Go give him courteous conduct to this place. —
Mean time, the court shall hear Bellario's letter.

   Clerk. [Reads] '*Your grace shall understand that
at the receipt of your letter I am very sick; but in the
instant that your messenger came, in loving visitation
was with me a young doctor of Rome; his name is
Balthasar. I acquainted him with the cause in controversy between the Jew and Antonio the merchant;* 150
*we turned o'er many books together. He is furnished
with my opinion, which, bettered with his own learning,
the greatness whereof I cannot enough commend, comes
with him, at my importunity, to fill up your grace's
request in my stead. I beseech you, let his lack of years
be no impediment to let him lack a reverend estimation;
for I never knew so young a body with so old a head.
I leave him to your gracious acceptance, whose trial
shall better publish his commendation.*'

   Duke. You hear the learn'd Bellario, what he writes; 160
And here, I take it, is the doctor come. —

      Enter PORTIA, *dressed like a doctor of laws*

Give me your hand.   Came you from old Bellario?

   Portia. I did, my lord.

Duke.   You are welcome; take your place.
Are you acquainted with the difference
That holds this present question in the court?
  Portia. I am informed throughly of the cause.
Which is the merchant here, and which the Jew?
  Duke. Antonio and old Shylock, both stand forth.
  Portia. Is your name Shylock?
  Shylock.   Shylock is my name.
  Portia. Of a strange nature is the suit you follow, 170
Yet in such rule that the Venetian law
Cannot impugn you as you do proceed. —
You stand within his danger, do you not?
  Antonio. Ay, so he says.
  Portia.   Do you confess the bond?
  Antonio. I do.
  Portia.   Then must the Jew be merciful.
  Shylock. On what compulsion must I? tell me that.
  Portia. The quality of mercy is not strain'd;
It droppeth as the gentle rain from heaven
Upon the place beneath. It is twice blest;
It blesseth him that gives and him that takes.   180
'T is mightiest in the mightiest; it becomes
The throned monarch better than his crown.
His sceptre shows the force of temporal power,
The attribute to awe and majesty,
Wherein doth sit the dread and fear of kings;
But mercy is above this sceptred sway;
It is enthroned in the hearts of kings,
It is an attribute to God himself;

And earthly power doth then show likest God's
When mercy seasons justice.   Therefore, Jew,   190
Though justice be thy plea, consider this, —
That, in the course of justice, none of us
Should see salvation; we do pray for mercy,
And that same prayer doth teach us all to render
The deeds of mercy.   I have spoke thus much
To mitigate the justice of thy plea,
Which if thou follow, this strict court of Venice
Must needs give sentence 'gainst the merchant there.

    Shylock.   My deeds upon my head !   I crave the law,
The penalty and forfeit of my bond.   200

    Portia.   Is he not able to discharge the money ?

    Bassanio.   Yes, here I tender it for him in the court ;
Yea, twice the sum.   If that will not suffice,
I will be bound to pay it ten times o'er,
On forfeit of my hands, my head, my heart ;
If this will not suffice, it must appear
That malice bears down truth.   And I beseech you,
Wrest once the law to your authority ;
To do a great right, do a little wrong,
And curb this cruel devil of his will.   210

    Portia.   It must not be.   There is no power in Venice
Can alter a decree established ;
'T will be recorded for a precedent,
And many an error by the same example
Will rush into the state.   It cannot be.

    Shylock.   A Daniel come to judgment ! yea, a Daniel !
O wise young judge, how do I honour thee !

Portia. I pray you, let me look upon the bond.

Shylock. Here 't is, most reverend doctor, here it is.

Portia. Shylock, there 's thrice thy money offer'd thee.

Shylock. An oath, an oath, I have an oath in heaven;
Shall I lay perjury upon my soul?   222
No, not for Venice.

Portia.   Why, this bond is forfeit;
And lawfully by this the Jew may claim
A pound of flesh, to be by him cut off
Nearest the merchant's heart. — Be merciful;
Take thrice thy money; bid me tear the bond.

Shylock. When it is paid according to the tenour. —
It doth appear you are a worthy judge;
You know the law; your exposition   230
Hath been most sound. I charge you by the law,
Whereof you are a well-deserving pillar,
Proceed to judgment. By my soul I swear,
There is no power in the tongue of man
To alter me. I stay here on my bond.

Antonio. Most heartily I do beseech the court
To give the judgment.

Portia.   Why then, thus it is:
You must prepare your bosom for his knife.

Shylock. O noble judge! O excellent young man!

Portia. For the intent and purpose of the law   240
Hath full relation to the penalty,
Which here appeareth due upon the bond.

Shylock. 'T is very true. O wise and upright judge!
How much more elder art thou than thy looks!

Portia. Therefore lay bare your bosom.

Shylock.   Ay, his breast;
So says the bond — doth it not, noble judge? —
Nearest his heart; those are the very words.

Portia. It is so.   Are there balance here to weigh
      the flesh?

Shylock. I have them ready.

Portia. Have by some surgeon, Shylock, on your
      charge,   250
To stop his wounds, lest he do bleed to death.

Shylock. Is it so nominated in the bond?

Portia. It is not so express'd; but what of that?
'T were good you do so much for charity.

Shylock. I cannot find it; 't is not in the bond.

Portia. You, merchant, have you any thing to say?

Antonio. But little; I am arm'd and well prepar'd. —
Give me your hand, Bassanio; fare you well!
Grieve not that I am fallen to this for you;
For herein Fortune shows herself more kind   260
Than is her custom.   It is still her use
To let the wretched man outlive his wealth,
To view with hollow eye and wrinkled brow
An age of poverty; from which lingering penance
Of such misery doth she cut me off.
Commend me to your honourable wife.
Tell her the process of Antonio's end;
Say how I lov'd you, speak me fair in death,
And when the tale is told bid her be judge
Whether Bassanio had not once a love.   270

Repent not you that you shall lose your friend,
And he repents not that he pays your debt;
For if the Jew do cut but deep enough,
I 'll pay it instantly with all my heart.

   Bassanio. Antonio, I am married to a wife
Which is as dear to me as life itself;
But life itself, my wife, and all the world,
Are not with me esteem'd above thy life.
I would lose all, ay, sacrifice them all
Here to this devil, to deliver you.   280

   Portia. Your wife would give you little thanks for that,
If she were by to hear you make the offer.

   Gratiano. I have a wife, whom, I protest, I love;
I would she were in heaven, so she could
Entreat some power to change this currish Jew.

   Nerissa. 'T is well you offer it behind her back;
The wish would make else an unquiet house.

   Shylock. [*Aside*] These be the Christian husbands.
     I have a daughter;
Would any of the stock of Barrabas
Had been her husband rather than a Christian!—   290
[*To Portia*] We trifle time; I pray thee, pursue sentence.

   Portia. A pound of that same merchant's flesh is
     thine;
The court awards it, and the law doth give it.

   Shylock. Most rightful judge!

   Portia. And you must cut this flesh from off his
     breast;
The law allows it, and the court awards it.

Shylock. Most learned judge! — A sentence!   Come,
    prepare!
Portia. Tarry a little; there is something else.
This bond doth give thee here no jot of blood;
The words expressly are, a pound of flesh.   300
Take then thy bond, take thou thy pound of flesh;
But, in the cutting it, if thou dost shed
One drop of Christian blood, thy lands and goods
Are, by the laws of Venice, confiscate
Unto the state of Venice.
    Gratiano. O upright judge! — Mark, Jew! — O
        learned judge!
Shylock. Is that the law?
Portia.   Thyself shalt see the act;
For, as thou urgest justice, be assur'd
Thou shalt have justice, more than thou desirest.
    Gratiano. O learned judge! — Mark Jew! — a learned
        judge!   310
    Shylock. I take this offer, then; pay the bond thrice,
And let the Christian go.
    Bassanio.   Here is the money.
    Portia. Soft!
The Jew shall have all justice; — soft! no haste: —
He shall have nothing but the penalty.
    Gratiano. O Jew! an upright judge, a learned judge!
    Portia. Therefore prepare thee to cut off the flesh.
Shed thou no blood, nor cut thou less nor more
But just a pound of flesh; if thou tak'st more
Or less than a just pound, be it but so much   320

As makes it light or heavy in the substance,
Or the division of the twentieth part
Of one poor scruple — nay, if the scale do turn
But in the estimation of a hair,
Thou diest, and all thy goods are confiscate.

   Gratiano. A second Daniel, a Daniel, Jew !
Now, infidel, I have thee on the hip.

   Portia. Why doth the Jew pause ? — Take thy forfeiture.

   Shylock. Give me my principal, and let me go.

   Bassanio. I have it ready for thee ; here it is.   330

   Portia. He hath refus'd it in the open court ;
He shall have merely justice and his bond.

   Gratiano. A Daniel, still say I, a second Daniel !
I thank thee, Jew, for teaching me that word.

   Shylock. Shall I not have barely my principal ?

   Portia. Thou shalt have nothing but the forfeiture,
To be so taken at thy peril, Jew.

   Shylock. Why, then the devil give him good of it !
I 'll stay no longer question.

   Portia.   Tarry, Jew ;
The law hath yet another hold on you.   340
It is enacted in the laws of Venice,
If it be prov'd against an alien
That by direct or indirect attempts
He seek the life of any citizen,
The party 'gainst the which he doth contrive
Shall seize one half his goods ; the other half
Comes to the privy coffer of the state ;

And the offender's life lies in the mercy
Of the duke only, 'gainst all other voice.
In which predicament, I say, thou stand'st ;   350
For it appears, by manifest proceeding,
That indirectly, and directly too,
Thou hast contriv'd against the very life
Of the defendant, and thou hast incurr'd
The danger formerly by me rehears'd.
Down therefore, and beg mercy of the duke.

    Gratiano. Beg that thou mayst have leave to hang
        thyself:
And yet, thy wealth being forfeit to the state,
Thou hast not left the value of a cord ;
Therefore thou must be hang'd at the state's charge. 360

    Duke. That thou shalt see the difference of our spirits,
I pardon thee thy life before thou ask it.
For half thy wealth, it is Antonio's ;
The other half comes to the general state,
Which humbleness may drive unto a fine.

    Portia. Ay, for the state, not for Antonio.

    Shylock. Nay, take my life and all ; pardon not that.
You take my house when you do take the prop
That doth sustain my house ; you take my life
When you do take the means whereby I live.   370

    Portia. What mercy can you render him, Antonio ?

    Gratiano. A halter gratis ; nothing else, for God's sake.

    Antonio. So please my lord the duke and all the court
To quit the fine for one half of his goods,
I am content, so he will let me have

The other half in use, to render it,
Upon his death, unto the gentleman
That lately stole his daughter.
Two things provided more, — that, for this favour,
He presently become a Christian;　　　　　　380
The other, that he do record a gift,
Here in the court, of all he dies possess'd,
Unto his son Lorenzo and his daughter.

Duke. He shall do this, or else I do recant
The pardon that I late pronounced here.

Portia. Art thou contented, Jew? what dost thou say?

Shylock. I am content.

Portia.　　　　　　Clerk, draw a deed of gift.

Shylock. I pray you, give me leave to go from hence;
I am not well. Send the deed after me,
And I will sign it.

Duke.　　　　Get thee gone, but do it.　　390

Gratiano. In christening thou shalt have two god-
　　　　fathers;
Had I been judge, thou shouldst have had ten more,
To bring thee to the gallows, not the font. [*Exit Shylock.*

Duke. Sir, I entreat you home with me to dinner.

Portia. I humbly do desire your grace of pardon;
I must away this night toward Padua,
And it is meet I presently set forth.

Duke. I am sorry that your leisure serves you not. —
Antonio, gratify this gentleman,
For, in my mind, you are much bound to him.　　400
　　　　　　　　[*Exeunt Duke and his train.*

Bassanio. Most worthy gentleman, I and my friend
Have by your wisdom been this day acquitted
Of grievous penalties; in lieu whereof
Three thousand ducats, due unto the Jew,
We freely cope your courteous pains withal.

Antonio. And stand indebted, over and above,
In love and service to you evermore.

Portia. He is well paid that is well satisfied;
And I, delivering you, am satisfied,
And therein do account myself well paid.   410
My mind was never yet more mercenary.
I pray you, know me when we meet again;
I wish you well, and so I take my leave.

Bassanio. Dear sir, of force I must attempt you
        further.
Take some remembrance of us, as a tribute,
Not as a fee; grant me two things, I pray you,
Not to deny me, and to pardon me.

Portia. You press me far, and therefore I will yield. —
[*To Antonio*] Give me your gloves, I'll wear them for
        your sake; —
[*To Bassanio*] And, for your love, I'll take this ring
        from you. —   420
Do not draw back your hand; I'll take no more,
And you in love shall not deny me this.

Bassanio. This ring, good sir, — alas! it is a trifle;
I will not shame myself to give you this.

Portia. I will have nothing else but only this;
And now methinks I have a mind to it.

Bassanio. There's more depends on this than on the
    value.
The dearest ring in Venice will I give you,
And find it out by proclamation;
Only for this, I pray you, pardon me.   430
  Portia. I see, sir, you are liberal in offers;
You taught me first to beg, and now methinks
You teach me how a beggar should be answer'd.
  Bassanio. Good sir, this ring was given me by my
    wife;
And when she put it on she made me vow
That I should neither sell, nor give, nor lose it.
  Portia. That 'scuse serves many men to save their
    gifts;
And if your wife be not a mad woman,
And know how well I have deserv'd the ring,
She would not hold out enemy for ever,   440
For giving it to me.   Well, peace be with you!
                [Exeunt Portia and Nerissa.
  Antonio. My lord Bassanio, let him have the ring;
Let his deservings and my love withal
Be valued 'gainst your wife's commandement.
  Bassanio. Go, Gratiano, run and overtake him;
Give him the ring, and bring him, if thou canst,
Unto Antonio's house.   Away! make haste.—
                    [Exit Gratiano.
Come, you and I will thither presently;
And in the morning early will we both
Fly toward Belmont.   Come, Antonio.   *[Exeunt.* 450

SCENE II.   *The Same.   A Street*

Enter PORTIA *and* NERISSA

Portia. Inquire the Jew's house out, give him this
     deed,
And let him sign it; we 'll away to-night,
And be a day before our husbands home.
This deed will be well welcome to Lorenzo.

Enter GRATIANO

Gratiano. Fair sir, you are well o'erta'en;
My lord Bassanio, upon more advice,
Hath sent you here this ring, and doth entreat
Your company at dinner.
Portia.   That cannot be.
His ring I do accept most thankfully,
And so, I pray you, tell him; furthermore,   10
I pray you, show my youth old Shylock's house.
Gratiano. That will I do.
Nerissa.   Sir, I would speak with you. —
[*Aside to Portia*] I 'll see if I can get my husband's ring,
Which I did make him swear to keep for ever.
Portia. [*Aside to Nerissa*] Thou mayst, I warrant.
     We shall have old swearing
That they did give the rings away to men;
But we 'll outface them, and outswear them too.
Away! make haste; thou know'st where I will tarry.
Nerissa. Come, good sir, will you show me to this
     house?   [*Exeunt.*

GARDEN SCENE

ACT V

SCENE I. *Belmont. Avenue to Portia's House*

Enter LORENZO *and* JESSICA

Lorenzo. The moon shines bright. In such a night
    as this,
When the sweet wind did gently kiss the trees
And they did make no noise — in such a night,
Troilus methinks mounted the Trojan walls,
And sigh'd his soul toward the Grecian tents,
Where Cressid lay that night.

Jessica.   In such a night,
Did Thisbe fearfully o'ertrip the dew,
And saw the lion's shadow ere himself,
And ran dismay'd away.

Lorenzo.   In such a night,
Stood Dido with a willow in her hand   10
Upon the wild sea banks, and waft her love
To come again to Carthage.

Jessica.   In such a night,
Medea gather'd the enchanted herbs
That did renew old Æson.

Lorenzo.   In such a night,
Did Jessica steal from the wealthy Jew,
And with an unthrift love did run from Venice
As far as Belmont.

Jessica.   In such a night,
Did young Lorenzo swear he lov'd her well,
Stealing her soul with many vows of faith,
And ne'er a true one.

Lorenzo.   In such a night,   20
Did pretty Jessica, like a little shrew,
Slander her love, and he forgave it her.

Jessica. I would out-night you, did nobody come ;
But, hark, I hear the footing of a man.

Enter STEPHANO

Lorenzo. Who comes so fast in silence of the night ?
Stephano. A friend.

Lorenzo. A friend! what friend? your name, I pray
    you, friend?

Stephano. Stephano is my name, and I bring word
My mistress will before the break of day
Be here at Belmont; she doth stray about   30
By holy crosses, where she kneels and prays
For happy wedlock hours.

Lorenzo.   Who comes with her?

Stephano. None but a holy hermit and her maid.
I pray you, is my master yet return'd?

Lorenzo. He is not, nor we have not heard from
    him. —
But go we in, I pray thee, Jessica,
And ceremoniously let us prepare
Some welcome for the mistress of the house.

Enter LAUNCELOT

Launcelot. Sola, sola! wo ha, ho! sola, sola!

Lorenzo. Who calls?   40

Launcelot. Sola! did you see Master Lorenzo and
Mistress Lorenzo? sola, sola!

Lorenzo. Leave hollaing, man; here.

Launcelot. Sola! where? where?

Lorenzo. Here.

Launcelot. Tell him there's a post come from my
master, with his horn full of good news; my master will
be here ere morning.   [*Exit.*

Lorenzo. Sweet soul, let's in, and there expect their
    coming.

And yet no matter; why should we go in?—   50
My friend Stephano, signify, I pray you,
Within the house, your mistress is at hand;
And bring your music forth into the air.—

                                    [*Exit Stephano.*

How sweet the moonlight sleeps upon this bank!
Here will we sit and let the sounds of music
Creep in our ears; soft stillness and the night
Become the touches of sweet harmony.
Sit, Jessica.   Look how the floor of heaven
Is thick inlaid with patines of bright gold.
There 's not the smallest orb which thou behold'st   60
But in his motion like an angel sings,
Still quiring to the young-eyed cherubins;
Such harmony is in immortal souls,
But whilst this muddy vesture of decay
Doth grossly close it in, we cannot hear it.—

Enter Musicians

Come, ho! and wake Diana with a hymn;
With sweetest touches pierce your mistress' ear,
And draw her home with music.   [*Music.*
    Jessica. I am never merry when I hear sweet music.
    Lorenzo. The reason is, your spirits are attentive.   70
For do but note a wild and wanton herd,
Or race of youthful and unhandled colts,
Fetching mad bounds, bellowing and neighing loud,
Which is the hot condition of their blood;
If they but hear perchance a trumpet sound,

Or any air of music touch their ears,
You shall perceive them make a mutual stand,
Their savage eyes turn'd to a modest gaze
By the sweet power of music.   Therefore the poet
Did feign that Orpheus drew trees, stones, and floods; 80
Since nought so stockish, hard, and full of rage,
But music for the time doth change his nature.
The man that hath no music in himself,
Nor is not mov'd with concord of sweet sounds,
Is fit for treasons, stratagems, and spoils;
The motions of his spirit are dull as night,
And his affections dark as Erebus.
Let no such man be trusted. — Mark the music.

Enter PORTIA *and* NERISSA

   Portia. That light we see is burning in my hall.
How far that little candle throws his beams! 90
So shines a good deed in a naughty world.
   Nerissa. When the moon shone, we did not see the
     candle.
   Portia. So doth the greater glory dim the less;
A substitute shines brightly as a king
Until a king be by, and then his state
Empties itself, as doth an inland brook
Into the main of waters. — Music! hark!
   Nerissa. It is your music, madam, of the house.
   Portia. Nothing is good, I see, without respect;
Methinks it sounds much sweeter than by day. 100
   Nerissa. Silence bestows that virtue on it, madam.

Portia. The crow doth sing as sweetly as the lark
When neither is attended ; and I think
The nightingale, if she should sing by day
When every goose is cackling, would be thought
No better a musician than the wren.
How many things by season season'd are
To their right praise and true perfection ! —
Peace, ho ! the moon sleeps with Endymion,
And would not be awak'd.   [*Music ceases.*

Lorenzo.   That is the voice,   110
Or I am much deceiv'd, of Portia.

Portia. He knows me as the blind man knows the
          cuckoo,
By the bad voice.

Lorenzo.   Dear lady, welcome home.

Portia. We have been praying for our husbands'
          welfare,
Which speed, we hope, the better for our words.
Are they return'd ?

Lorenzo.   Madam, they are not yet ;
But there is come a messenger before,
To signify their coming.

Portia.   Go in, Nerissa ;
Give order to my servants that they take
No note at all of our being absent hence ; —   120
Nor you, Lorenzo ; — Jessica, nor you. [*A tucket sounds.*

Lorenzo. Your husband is at hand ; I hear his trumpet.
We are no tell-tales, madam ; fear you not.

Portia. This night methinks is but the daylight sick,

It looks a little paler; 't is a day
Such as the day is when the sun is hid.

Enter BASSANIO, ANTONIO, GRATIANO, *and their
followers*

Bassanio. We should hold day with the Antipodes
If you would walk in absence of the sun.

Portia. Let me give light, but let me not be light;
For a light wife doth make a heavy husband,   130
And never be Bassanio so for me.
But God sort all! You are welcome home, my lord.

Bassanio. I thank you, madam. Give welcome to
      my friend.
This is the man, this is Antonio,
To whom I am so infinitely bound.

Portia. You should in all sense be much bound to him,
For, as I hear, he was much bound for you.

Antonio. No more than I am well acquitted of.

Portia. Sir, you are very welcome to our house;
It must appear in other ways than words,   140
Therefore I scant this breathing courtesy.

Gratiano. [*To Nerissa*] By yonder moon I swear you
      do me wrong;
In faith, I gave it to the judge's clerk.

Portia. A quarrel, ho, already! what 's the matter?

Gratiano. About a hoop of gold, a paltry ring
That she did give me, whose poesy was
For all the world like cutler's poetry
Upon a knife, 'Love me, and leave me not.'

Nerissa. What talk you of the poesy or the value?
You swore to me, when I did give it you,   150
That you would wear it till the hour of death,
And that it should lie with you in your grave;
Though not for me, yet for your vehement oaths,
You should have been respective and have kept it.
Gave it a judge's clerk! but well I know
The clerk will ne'er wear hair on 's face that had it.

Gratiano. He will, an if he live to be a man.

Nerissa. Ay, if a woman live to be a man.

Gratiano. Now, by this hand, I gave it to a youth,
A kind of boy, a little scrubbed boy,   160
No higher than thyself, the judge's clerk,
A prating boy, that begg'd it as a fee;
I could not for my heart deny it him.

Portia. You were to blame, I must be plain with you,
To part so slightly with your wife's first gift;
A thing stuck on with oaths upon your finger,
And so riveted with faith unto your flesh.
I gave my love a ring, and made him swear
Never to part with it; and here he stands.
I dare be sworn for him, he would not leave it,   170
Nor pluck it from his finger, for the wealth
That the world masters.   Now, in faith, Gratiano,
You give your wife too unkind a cause of grief;
An 't were to me, I should be mad at it.

Bassanio. [*Aside*] Why, I were best to cut my left
        hand off,
And swear I lost the ring defending it.

Gratiano. My lord Bassanio gave his ring away
Unto the judge that begg'd it, and indeed
Deserv'd it too ; and then the boy, his clerk,
That took some pains in writing, he begg'd mine ;   180
And neither man nor master would take aught
But the two rings.
    Portia.   What ring gave you, my lord ?
Not that, I hope, which you receiv'd of me.
    Bassanio. If I could add a lie unto a fault,
I would deny it, but you see my finger
Hath not the ring upon it ; it is gone.
    Portia. Even so void is your false heart of truth.
By heaven, I will ne'er come in your bed
Until I see the ring.
    Nerissa.   Nor I in yours
Till I again see mine.
    Bassanio.   Sweet Portia,   190
If you did know to whom I gave the ring,
If you did know for whom I gave the ring,
And would conceive for what I gave the ring,
And how unwillingly I left the ring,
When nought would be accepted but the ring,
You would abate the strength of your displeasure.
    Portia. If you had known the virtue of the ring,
Or half her worthiness that gave the ring,
Or your own honour to contain the ring,
You would not then have parted with the ring.   200
What man is there so much unreasonable,
If you had pleas'd to have defended it

With any terms of zeal, wanted the modesty
To urge the thing held as a ceremony?
Nerissa teaches me what to believe;
I 'll die for 't but some woman had the ring.

    Bassanio. No, by my honour, madam, by my soul,
No woman had it, but a civil doctor,
Which did refuse three thousand ducats of me,
And begg'd the ring; the which I did deny him,   210
And suffer'd him to go displeas'd away,
Even he that did uphold the very life
Of my dear friend.   What should I say, sweet lady?
I was enforc'd to send it after him;
I was beset with shame and courtesy;
My honour would not let ingratitude
So much besmear it.   Pardon me, good lady;
For, by these blessed candles of the night,
Had you been there, I think you would have begg'd
The ring of me to give the worthy doctor.   220

    Portia. Let not that doctor e'er come near my
        house.
Since he hath got the jewel that I lov'd,
And that which you did swear to keep for me,
I will become as liberal as you;
I 'll not deny him any thing I have.

    Antonio. I am the unhappy subject of these quarrels.

    Portia. Sir, grieve not you; you are welcome not-
        withstanding.

    Bassanio. Portia, forgive me this enforced wrong;
And, in the hearing of these many friends,

I swear to thee, even by thine own fair eyes, 230
Wherein I see myself, —

   Portia.   Mark you but that !
In both my eyes he doubly sees himself ;
In each eye, one ! — Swear by your double self,
And there 's an oath of credit.

   Bassanio.   Nay, but hear me :
Pardon this fault, and by my soul I swear
I never more will break an oath with thee.

   Antonio. I once did lend my body for his wealth,
Which, but for him that had your husband's ring,
Had quite miscarried ; I dare be bound again,
My soul upon the forfeit, that your lord 240
Will never more break faith advisedly.

   Portia. Then you shall be his surety. Give him this,
And bid him keep it better than the other.

   Antonio. Here, lord Bassanio ; swear to keep this ring.

   Bassanio. By heaven, it is the same I gave the doctor !

   Portia. You are all amaz'd.
Here is a letter, read it at your leisure ;
It comes from Padua, from Bellario.
There you shall find that Portia was the doctor,
Nerissa there her clerk. Lorenzo here 250
Shall witness I set forth as soon as you,
And even but now return'd ; I have not yet
Enter'd my house. — Antonio, you are welcome ;
And I have better news in store for you
Than you expect. Unseal this letter soon ;
There you shall find, three of your argosies

Are richly come to harbour suddenly.
You shall not know by what strange accident
I chanced on this letter.

   Antonio. Sweet lady, you have given me life and
      living;   260
For here I read for certain that my ships
Are safely come to road.

   Portia.   How now, Lorenzo?
My clerk hath some good comforts too for you.

   Nerissa. Ay, and I 'll give them him without a fee. —
There do I give to you and Jessica,
From the rich Jew, a special deed of gift,
After his death, of all he dies possess'd of.

   Lorenzo. Fair ladies, you drop manna in the way
Of starved people.

   Portia.   It is almost morning,
And yet I am sure you are not satisfied   270
Of these events at full.   Let us go in;
And charge us there upon inter'gatories,
And we will answer all things faithfully   [*Exeunt.*

NOTES

THE CASKETS

NOTES

INTRODUCTION

THE METRE OF THE PLAY. — It should be understood at the outset that *metre*, or the mechanism of verse, is something altogether distinct from the *music* of verse. The one is matter of rule, the other of taste and feeling. Music is not an absolute necessity of verse; the metrical form is a necessity, being that which constitutes the verse.

The plays of Shakespeare (with the exception of rhymed passages, and of occasional songs and interludes) are all in unrhymed or *blank* verse; and the normal form of this blank verse is illustrated by the first line of the present play: "In sooth, I know not why I am so sad."

This line, it will be seen, consists of ten syllables, with the even syllables (2d, 4th, 6th, 8th, and 10th) accented, the odd syllables (1st, 3d, etc.) being unaccented. Theoretically, it is made up of five *feet* of two syllables each, with the accent on the second syllable. Such a foot is called an *iambus* (plural, *iambuses*, or the Latin *iambi*), and the form of verse is called *iambic*.

This fundamental law of Shakespeare's verse is subject to certain modifications, the most important of which are as follows: —

1. After the tenth syllable an unaccented syllable (or even two such syllables) may be added, forming what is sometimes called a *female* line; as in the third line of the first scene: "But how I caught it, found it, or came by it." The rhythm is complete with *by*, the *it* being an extra eleventh syllable. In line 69, we have two extra syllables, the rhythm being complete with the second syllable of *Antonio*.

2. The accent in any part of the verse may be shifted from an even to an odd syllable; as in lines 18, 19: —

> "Plucking the grass, to know where sits the wind,
> Peering in maps for ports and piers and roads."

In both lines the accent is shifted from the second to the first syllable. This change occurs very rarely in the tenth syllable, and seldom in the fourth; and it is not allowable in two successive accented syllables.

3. An extra unaccented syllable may occur in any part of the line; as in lines 29, 47, and 48. In 29 the second syllable of *burial* is superfluous; in 47 the word *us ;* and in 48 the second syllable of *merry*. Line 48 has also the unaccented final syllable in *easy*, making it a female line.

4. Any unaccented syllable, occurring in an even place immediately before or after an even syllable which is properly accented, is reckoned as accented for the purposes of the verse; as, for instance, in lines 12 and 13. In 12 the first syllable of *overpeer* and the last of *traffickers* are metrically equivalent to accented syllables; and so

with the last syllable of *reverence* in 13. Other examples are the last syllable of *Antonio* in lines 39, 73, 122, and 130, and that of *Portia* in 166. In 166 *Portia* must be made distinctly a trisyllable (as in ii. 7. 43 and 47), but in 165 (as often) it is virtually a dissyllable.

5. In many instances in Shakespeare words must be *lengthened* in order to fill out the rhythm : —

(*a*) In a large class of words in which *e* or *i* is followed by another vowel, the *e* or *i* is made a separate syllable; as *ocean, opinion, soldier, patience, partial, marriage*, etc. For instance, line 8 of the first scene of the present play appears to have only nine syllables, but *ocean* (see note on the word) is a trisyllable. In 102 *opinion* is a quadrisyllable (but a trisyllable in 91); *occasions* has five syllables in 139; and many similar instances are mentioned in the Notes. This lengthening occurs most frequently at the end of the line.

(*b*) Many monosyllables ending in *r, re, rs, res*, preceded by a long vowel or diphthong, are often made dissyllables; as *fare, fear, dear, fire, hair, hour, your*, etc. In iii. 2. 297 : "Shall lose a hair through Bassanio's fault," *hair* is a dissyllable. If the word is repeated in a verse it is often both monosyllable and dissyllable; as in iii. 2. 20 : "And so, though yours, not yours. Prove it so," where either *yours* (preferably the first) is a dissyllable, the other being a monosyllable. In *J. C.* iii. 1. 172 : "As fire drives out fire, so pity, pity," the first *fire* is a dissyllable.

(*c*) Words containing *l* or *r*, preceded by another consonant, are often pronounced as if a vowel came between the consonants; as in *T. of S.* ii. 1. 158 : "While she did call me rascal fiddler" [fidd(e)ler]; *All's Well*, iii. 5. 43 : "If you will tarry, holy pilgrim" [pilg(e)rim]; *C. of E.* v. 1. 360 : "These are the parents of these children" [childeren, the original form of the word]; *W. T.* iv. 4. 76 : "Grace and remembrance [rememb(e)rance] be to you both !" etc.

(*d*) Monosyllabic exclamations (*ay, O, yea, nay, hail,* etc.) and monosyllables otherwise emphasized are similarly lengthened; also certain longer words; as *commandement* in the present play (iv. i. 444); *safety* (trisyllable) in *Ham.* i. 3. 21; *business* (trisyllable, as originally pronounced) in *J. C.* iv. 1. 22: "To groan and sweat under the business" (so in several other passages); and other words mentioned in the notes to the plays in which they occur.

6. Words are also *contracted* for metrical reasons, like plurals and possessives ending in a sibilant, as *balance* (see note on iv. 1. 248), *horse* (for *horses* and *horse's*), *princess*, *sense*, *marriage* (plural and possessive), *image*, etc. So *spirit* (see note on ii. 2. 189), *inter'gatories* (see on v. 1. 272), *unpleasant'st* (see on iii. 2. 246), and other words mentioned in the notes on this and other plays.

7. The *accent* of words is also varied in many instances for metrical reasons. Thus we find both *révenue* and *revénue* in the first scene of the *M. N. D.* (lines 6 and 158), *òbscure* (see note on ii. 7. 51) and *obscùre*, *pùrsue* (see on iv. 1. 291) and *pursùe*, *dìstinct* (see on ii. 9. 60) and *distìnct*, etc.

These instances of variable accent must not be confounded with those in which words were uniformly accented differently in the time of Shakespeare; like *aspèct* (see on i. 1. 54), *impórtune*, *perséver* (never *persevère*), *perséverance*, *rheúmatic*, etc.

8. *Alexandrines*, or verses of twelve syllables, with six accents, occur here and there; as in the inscriptions on the caskets (and a few other instances) in this play. They must not be confounded with female lines with two extra syllables (see on 1 above) or with other lines in which two extra unaccented syllables may occur.

9. *Incomplete* verses, of one or more syllables, are scattered through the plays. See note on i. 1. 5 of this play.

10. *Doggerel* measure (i. 1. 111 and the last line of i. 2 in this play) is used in the very earliest comedies (*L. L. L.* and *C. of E.* in particular) in the mouths of comic characters, but nowhere else in those plays, and never anywhere after the date of the *Merchant*.

11. *Rhyme* occurs frequently in the early plays, but diminishes with comparative regularity from that period until the latest. Thus,

in *L. L. L.* there are about 1100 rhyming verses (about one-third of the whole number), in the *M. N. D.* about 900, in *Rich. II.* and *R. and J.* about 500 each, while in *Cor.* and *A. and C.* there are only about 40 each, in the *Temp.* only two, and in the *W. T.* none at all, except in the chorus introducing act iv. Songs, interludes, and other matter not in ten-syllable measure are not included in this enumeration. In the present play, out of some 2000 verses, less than a hundred are in rhyme.

Alternate rhymes are found only in the plays written before 1599 or 1600. In the *Merchant* there are only four lines — at the end of iii. 2. In *Much Ado* and *A. Y. L.* we also find a few lines, but none at all in subsequent plays.

Rhymed couplets, or "rhyme-tags," are often found at the end of scenes; as in the first scene, and twelve other scenes, of the present play. In *Ham.*, 14 out of 20 scenes, and in *Macb.*, 21 out of 28, have such "tags"; but in the latest plays they are not so frequent. The *Temp.*, for instance, has but one, and the *W. T.* none.

SHAKESPEARE'S USE OF VERSE AND PROSE IN THE PLAYS. — This is a subject to which the critics have given very little attention, but it is an interesting study. In the *Merchant* we find scenes entirely in verse or in prose, and others in which the two are mixed. In general, we may say that verse is used for what is distinctly poetical, and prose for what is not poetical. The distinction, however, is not so clearly marked in the earlier as in the later plays. The second scene of the *Merchant*, for instance, is in prose, because Portia and Nerissa are talking about the suitors in a familiar and playful way; but in the *T. G. of V.*, where Julia and Lucetta are discussing the suitors of the former in much the same fashion, the scene is all in verse. Dowden, commenting on *Rich. II.*, remarks: "Had Shakespeare written the play a few years later, we may be certain that the gardener and his servants (iii. 4) would not have uttered stately speeches in verse, but would have spoken homely prose, and that humour would have mingled with the pathos of the scene. The same remark may be made with reference to the subsequent scene (v. 5) in which his groom visits the dethroned king in the Tower." Comic characters and those in low life generally speak in prose in the later plays, as Dowden intimates, but in the very earliest ones doggerel verse is much used instead. See on 10 above.

The change from prose to verse is well illustrated in the third scene of the *Merchant*. It begins with plain prosaic talk about a business matter; but when Antonio enters, it rises at once to the higher level of poetry. The sight of Antonio reminds Shylock of his hatred of the Merchant, and the passion expresses itself in verse, the vernacular tongue of poetry. We have a similar change in the first scene of *J. C.*, where, after the quibbling "chaff" of the mechanics about their trades, the mention of Pompey reminds the Tribune of their plebeian fickleness, and his scorn and indignation flame out in most eloquent verse.

The reasons for the choice of prose or verse are not always so clear as in these instances. We are seldom puzzled to explain the prose, but not unfrequently we meet with verse where we might expect prose. As Professor Corson remarks (*Introduction to Shakespeare*, 1889), "Shakespeare adopted verse as the general tenor of his language, and therefore expressed much in verse that is within the capabilities of prose; in other words, his verse constantly encroaches upon the domain of prose, but his prose can never be said to encroach upon the domain of verse." If in rare instances we think we find exceptions to this latter statement, and prose actually seems to usurp the place of verse, I believe that careful study of the passage will prove the supposed exception to be apparent rather than real.

SOME BOOKS FOR TEACHERS AND STUDENTS. — A few out of the many books that might be commended to the teacher and the critical student are the following: Halliwell-Phillipps's *Outlines of the Life of Shakespeare* (7th ed. 1887); Sidney Lee's *Life of Shakespeare* (1898; for ordinary students the abridged ed. of 1899 is preferable); Schmidt's *Shakespeare Lexicon* (3d ed. 1902);

Littledale's ed. of Dyce's *Glossary* (1902); Bartlett's *Concordance to Shakespeare* (1895); Abbott's *Shakespearian Grammar* (1873); Furness's "New Variorum" ed. of *The Merchant of Venice* (1888, encyclopædic and exhaustive); Dowden's *Shakspere: His Mind and Art* (American ed. 1881); Hudson's *Life, Art, and Characters of Shakespeare* (revised ed. 1882); Mrs. Jameson's *Characteristics of Women* (several eds., some with the title, *Shakespeare Heroines*); Ten Brink's *Five Lectures on Shakespeare* (1895); Boas's *Shakespeare and His Predecessors* (1895); Dyer's *Folk-lore of Shakespeare* (American ed. 1884); Gervinus's *Shakespeare Commentaries* (Bunnett's translation, 1875); Wordsworth's *Shakespeare's Knowledge of the Bible* (3d ed. 1880); Elson's *Shakespeare in Music* (1901).

Some of the above books will be useful to all readers who are interested in special subjects or in general criticism of Shakespeare. Among those which are better suited to the needs of ordinary readers and students, the following may be mentioned: Phin's *Cyclopædia and Glossary of Shakespeare* (1902, more compact and cheaper than Dyce); Dowden's *Shakspere Primer* (1877, small but invaluable); Rolfe's *Shakespeare the Boy* (1896, treating of the home and school life, the games and sports, the manners, customs, and folk-lore of the poet's time); Guerber's *Myths of Greece and Rome* (for young students who may need information on mythological allusions not explained in the notes).

Black's *Judith Shakespeare* (1884, a novel, but a careful study of the scene and the time) is a book that I always commend to young people, and their elders will also enjoy it. The Lambs' *Tales from Shakespeare* is a classic for beginners in the study of the dramatist; and in Rolfe's ed. the plan of the authors is carried out in the Notes by copious illustrative quotations from the plays. Mrs. Cowden-Clarke's *Girlhood of Shakespeare's Heroines* (several eds.) will particularly interest girls; and both girls and boys will find Bennett's *Master Skylark* (1897) and Imogen Clark's *Will Shakespeare's Little Lad* (1897) equally entertaining and instructive.

H. Snowden Ward's *Shakespeare's Town and Times* (1896) and John Leyland's *Shakespeare Country* (1900) are copiously illustrated books (yet inexpensive) which may be particularly commended for school libraries.

It is proper to add that certain books specially useful in the study of other plays than the *Merchant* are not included in the above lists.

ABBREVIATIONS IN THE NOTES. — The abbreviations of the names of Shakespeare's plays will be readily understood; as *T. N.* for *Twelfth Night*, *Cor.* for *Coriolanus*, *3 Hen. VI.* for *The Third Part of King Henry the Sixth*, etc. *P. P.* refers to *The Passionate Pilgrim; V. and A.* to *Venus and Adonis; L. C.* to *Lover's Complaint;* and *Sonn.* to the *Sonnets*.

Other abbreviations that hardly need explanation are *Cf.* (*confer*, compare), *Fol.* (following), *Id.* (*idem*, the same), and *Prol.* (prologue). The numbers of the lines in the references (except for the present play) are those of the "Globe" edition (the cheapest and best edition of *Shakespeare* in one compact volume), which is now generally accepted as the standard for line numbers in works of reference (Schmidt's *Lexicon*, Abbott's *Grammar*, Dowden's *Primer*, the publications of the New Shakspere Society, etc.).

ACT I

SCENE I. — In the first folio the play is divided into acts, but not into scenes, and there is no list of *dramatis personæ*. The quartos have no such list, and no division at all.

This scene, like many in this play (i. 3, ii. 1, 3, 4, 5, 8, etc.) and others, begins abruptly, the dialogue being already in progress. Here Antonio's friends have evidently been trying to find out why he is so melancholy. He says that he cannot explain it himself;

and the critics are puzzled by it.   For myself, I have no doubt that it is due to an indefinable presentiment of coming misfortune. Shakespeare, whether he believed in such premonitions or not, understood their dramatic value and often introduces them most effectively.   It has been objected, in the present instance, that "this play is not a tragedy, but a comedy, wherein a tragic keynote would be falsely struck."   But it comes perilously near proving a tragedy.   Antonio suffers all the pangs of death except the last and least, and the shadow of that impending sorrow may already rest upon him.   No other explanation of the passage that has been suggested seems to me so simple and satisfactory.

1. *In sooth*.   In truth.   The word *sooth*, which survives in *sooth-sayer* (teller of hidden truth), seldom occurs in Shakespeare except in asseverations, like *in sooth, in good sooth, good sooth* (as in ii. 6. 42 below), etc.

5. *I am to learn*.   I have yet to find out.   These imperfect lines are not uncommon in the plays.

8. *On the ocean*.   *Ocean* here is a trisyllable ; as in 2 *Hen. IV*. iii. 1. 50: "The beachy girdle of the ocean."   Final syllables containing *e* or *i* followed by another vowel are often thus lengthened by Elizabethan and later poets.   Cf. *opinion*, in line 102 below; *complexion* in ii. 1. 1; *intermission* in iii. 2. 199; *description* in iii. 2. 296; *imposition* in iii. 4. 33; and other instances in the present play.   Such words are often emphatic, and the lengthening adds to the emphasis; as in *ocean, complexion*, etc.

9. *Argosies*.   Merchant vessels, large for that day, though not exceeding 200 tons.   The word (formerly supposed to be from the classical *Argo*) is from *Ragusa*, a port in Dalmatia, as the old forms, *ragosie, rhaguse, ragusye*, etc., indicate.

11. *Pageants*.   The word in S. means usually a theatrical exhibition, literal or figurative.   Originally it meant the movable theatres to which Dugdale (*Antiquities of Warwickshire*, 1656), in his description of the old plays at Coventry, refers as "theatres for the principal scenes, very large and high, placed upon wheels, and

drawn to all the eminent parts of the city for the better advantage of spectators."

12. *Overpeer.* Tower above; as in 3 *Hen. VI.* v. 2. 14: " Whose top-branch overpeer'd Jove's spreading tree."

13. *Curtsy.* The same word as *courtesy;* used of both sexes in this sense.

15. *Venture.* Still used in this commercial sense. *Forth =* abroad.

17. *Still.* Ever, constantly, as in 136 below. On *plucking the grass,* etc., Ascham (*Toxophilus*) frequently refers to holding up " a fether or a lytle lyght grasse," to learn " how the wynd stoode," as boys sometimes do nowadays.

27. *My wealthy Andrew.* My richly freighted ship. Some suppose the name to be taken from that of the famous Genoese admiral, Andrea Doria, who died 1560.

28. *Vailing.* Lowering. Cf. " Vail your regard " (= let fall your look), *M. for M.* v. 1. 20, etc. The word is contracted from *avail* or *avale,* the French *avaler* (from Latin *ad vallem*). Editors and critics have sometimes confounded it with *veil.*

29. *Her burial.* That is, her burial place.

35. *But even now worth this.* The force of *this* (= all this, so much) was doubtless meant to be expressed by a gesture — perhaps a sweep of the right arm. Cf. *J. C.* iv. 3. 26: " For so much trash as may be grasped thus "; where *thus* is explained by closing the hand as if to hold the money.

40. *To think upon.* From thinking upon.

42. *Bottom.* This word, like *venture,* is still used in commerce in the same sense as here. Cf. *K. John,* ii. 1. 73 : " the English bottoms."

50. *Two-headed Janus.* In some of the ancient images of Janus a grave face was associated with a laughing one.

52. *Peep through their eyes.* That is, eyes half shut with laughter.

54. *Other of such vinegar aspect.* *Other* is often plural in S. and other writers of the time. *Aspect* is always accented on the last

syllable by S. and his contemporaries. Cf. Spenser, *F. Q.* i. 12. 23: "Most ugly shapes, and horrible aspects;" Milton, *P. L.* iii. 266: "His words here ended, but his meek aspect," etc.

56. *Nestor.* The oldest of the Greek heroes in the Iliad, famed for his wisdom and gravity. See *T. and C.*, in which he is a character.

61. *Prevented.* In its primitive sense of *anticipated.* Cf. *Ham.* ii. 2. 305, etc.; also *Psalms*, cxix. 147, and 1 *Thessalonians*, iv. 15.

62–64. *Your worth*, etc. This speech is characteristic of Antonio. He takes Salarino's conventional compliment to his friends too seriously.

67. *Exceeding strange.* S. often uses *exceeding* as an

TWO-HEADED JANUS

adverb. He uses *exceedingly* only five times — in four of which it modifies the adverb *well*, while in the fifth it modifies an adjective *understood.* *Exceeding strange* = our expression, "very much of a stranger."

74. *Respect upon the world.* Regard for the world.

78. *A stage.* Cf. the famous passage, "All the world's a stage," *A. Y. L.* ii. 7. 139 fol.

79. *Let me play the fool.* Let the part assigned to me be that of

the fool, who was always one of the characters in the old comedies. Cf. *2 Hen. IV*. ii. 2. 154: "thus we play the fools with the
time."

80. *Old wrinkles*. The wrinkles of age.

81. *Liver*. Cf. *A. and C*. ii. 1. 23: "I had rather heat my liver
with drinking."

82. *Than my heart cool*, etc. There may be an allusion here to
the old belief that every sigh or groan robbed the heart of a drop
of blood. Cf. *M. N. D*. iii. 2. 97: "Sighs of love that costs the
fresh blood dear."

84. *Alabaster*. All the early eds. have "alablaster," the more
common spelling in that day.

85. *Creep into the jaundice*. In the only other passage in which
S. mentions the jaundice, the cause of the disease is, as here, a
mental one. See *T. and C*. i. 3. 2.

89. *Do cream and mantle*. Cf. *Lear*, iii. 4. 139: "the green
mantle of the standing pool."

90. *And do a wilful stillness entertain*. And *who* do maintain
an obstinate silence. This kind of ellipsis is not uncommon when
the sense is clear.

91. *Opinion of wisdom*. Reputation for wisdom. *Opinion* is
here a trisyllable, but a quadrisyllable in 102 below.

92. *Conceit*. Intellect; as often.

93. *As who should say*. Like one who should say. The early
folios read, "I am sir an Oracle," which some editors prefer; but
cf. "Sir Prudence" (*Temp*. ii. 1. 286), "Sir Smile" (*W. T*. i. 2.
196), etc.

96. *That therefore only are reputed wise*, etc. That are reputed
wise only on this account, that they say nothing. Pope calls silence
"Thou varnisher of fools, and cheat of all the wise."

98. *Would almost*, etc. That is, *they* would; an ellipsis of the
nominative, as in 90 above. The meaning is that the hearers could
hardly help calling them fools, and thus exposing themselves to
the judgment threatened in Scripture (*Matthew*, v. 22).

101. *This melancholy bait.* This bait of melancholy; this melancholy as a bait.

102. *Fool gudgeon.* Old Izaak Walton says of the gudgeon : "It is an excellent fish to enter (initiate) a young angler, *being easy to be taken.*" On the adjective use of *fool*, cf. "fool multitude," ii. 9. 25 below.

108. *Moe.* More; used only with a plural or collective noun.

110. *For this gear.* For this purpose, or matter; an expression sometimes used, as here, without very definite meaning.

116. *You shall seek all day.* *Shall* and *should* are often used in all three persons, by the Elizabethan writers, to denote mere futurity.

124. *By something showing.* This adverbial use of *something* (= somewhat), which occurs twice in this speech, is common in S.

More swelling port. Grander state. Cf. "greatest port," iii. 2. 276 below.

125. *Would grant continuance.* That is, continuance *of.* Such ellipsis is common in the Elizabethan writers. Cf. ii. 6. 9 and iv. 1. 380 below.

126. *Make moan to be abridg'd.* Complain that I am curtailed. Cf. "made moan to me," iii. 3. 23 below.

129. *My time.* My time of life, my youth.

130. *Gag'd.* Engaged, bound.

136. *Still.* See on 17 above.

137. *Within the eye of honour.* Within the range of what can be viewed (or regarded) as honourable.

139. *Occasions.* Needs; here a quadrisyllable. See on 8 above.

141. *Flight.* A technical term to denote the range of an arrow. Cf. Ascham's *Toxophilus :* "You must have divers shafts of one flight, feathered with divers wings, for divers winds." *His = its,* which was then just coming into use. See on iii. 2. 82 below.

142. *More advised.* More careful. Cf. the modern use of *unadvised.*

143. *To find the other forth.* To find the other out. Cf. "to find his fellow forth," *C. of E.* i. 2. 37.

144. *Childhood proof.* Experiment of my childhood.

146. *Like a wilful youth.* Elliptical for "like what will happen with a wilful (that is, wilful in his prodigality) youth."

148. *That self way.* That same way. Cf. "this self place," 3 *Hen. VI.* iii. 1. 11; "that self mould," *Rich. II.* i. 2. 23, etc.

154. *Circumstance.* Circumlocution; as in *Ham.* i. 5. 127, etc.

156. *In making question*, etc. In doubting my readiness to do all that I can for you.

160. *Prest.* Ready; the old French *prest* (now *prêt*), Italian and Spanish *presto*, from Latin adv. *præsto*, through the late Latin *præstus.*

161. *Richly left.* Left rich. Cf. v. 1. 257: "richly come to harbour."

162. *And, fairer than that word.* Some take this as connected with what precedes and emphasizing *fair;* but it is clearly connected with what follows. Bassanio places her beauty above her wealth, and her virtues above her beauty. He had been acquainted with Portia in her father's time (i. 2. 112), before she came into her fortune, and began to love her then; and, as we see later, he did not misinterpret the "fair speechless messages" of her eyes. Lady Martin (*Some of Shakespeare's Female Characters*), commenting on the opening lines of the next scene, remarks: "Often, no doubt, has she wondered why he has not presented himself among her suitors. Unconsciously, perhaps, the languor of hope deferred speaks in these first words we hear from her. The one whom she thought might possibly have been among the first comers comes not at all."

163. *Sometimes.* In time past, formerly. *Sometimes* and *sometime* are used interchangeably by S. in this and their other senses.

165. *Nothing undervalued.* Nowise inferior. Cf. ii. 7. 53 below.

166. *Brutus' Portia.* See *J. C.*, in which this "woman well reputed, Cato's daughter," is a prominent character.

170. *Like a golden fleece,* etc. The Argonautic expedition is alluded to again, iii. 2. 236 below: " We are the Jasons, we have won the fleece."

175. *I have a mind presages.* That is, *which* presages. See on 90 above.

Thrift. Success. Cf. " well-won thrift " and " thrift is blessing," i. 3. 50, 86 below.

177, 178. *All my fortunes are at sea,* etc. This is not strictly consistent with 42–44 above; but S. is often careless in these minor matters.

Commodity. Property. In iii. 3. 27 below the word is used in the obsolete sense of *advantage* or *gain.* Cf. *W. T.* iii. 2. 94: " To me can life be no commodity."

183. *Presently.* Immediately. Cf. *Temp.* iv. 1. 42: "*Ariel.* Presently? *Prospero.* Ay, with a twink;" and again, v. 1. 101: "*Prospero.* And presently, I prithee. *Ariel.* I drink the air before me, and return Or ere your pulse beat twice." See also 1 *Samuel,* ii. 16, and *Matthew,* xxvi. 53.

185. *To have it of my trust,* etc. Of obtaining it either on my credit as a merchant, or as a personal favour.

Note the rhyme in the last couplet, as often at the close of a scene.

SCENE II. — 2. *Aweary.* A poetical form of *weary,* but occasionally used in prose, as here.

7. *It is no mean happiness.* So in the quartos. The folios have " no small happiness." The repetition is in Shakespeare's manner.

8. *Superfluity comes sooner by white hairs.* The rich are more likely to " live fast " and become prematurely old, and therefore to die the sooner.

26. *Nor refuse none.* This old double negative is common in S., and occasionally we find a triple one; as in *T. N.* iii. 1. 171: " nor never none," etc.

32. *But one who you shall rightly love. Who* is the object, not the subject, of *love,* as appears from the question which follows:

What affection have you for any of the suitors that are *already*
come? *Who* for *whom* is not unusual in the writers of the time.
Cf. ii. 6. 30 below.

36. *I pray thee, over-name them*, etc. The dialogue that follows
is an elaboration of the scene between Julia and Lucetta in *T. G.
of V.* i. 2.

38. *Level at.* Aim at, guess. Cf. *2 Hen. IV.* iii. 2. 286: "the
foeman may with as great aim level at the edge of a penknife."

41. *Makes it a great appropriation*, etc. That is, takes great
credit to himself for it. S. nowhere else uses either *appropriation*
or *appropriate*.

44. For *county* = count, see *R. and J.* (where it occurs eleven
times), *A. W.* iii. 7. 22, etc.

46. *An you will not.* The folio has "And you." *And* or *an*
for *if* is very common in old writers, as well as *and if* or *an if.
Choose;* that is, choose where you will; I don't care.

47. *The weeping philosopher.* Heracleitus, of Ephesus, who, from
his melancholy disposition, is represented in various old traditions
as the contrast to Democritus ("the laughing philosopher"), weeping over the frailties and follies at which the latter laughed.

49. *I had rather to be married. Had rather* and *had better* are
good English, though many writers of grammars tell us that we
should say *would rather*, etc., instead. *Rather* is the comparative
of *rath* (see Milton, *Lycidas:* "the rath primrose"), and is often
found in the old writers in the sense of *earlier, sooner.* Thus
Spenser, *Shep. Kal.* Feb., speaks of "the rather lambes." For *to*
after *had rather,* cf. *Oth.* i. 3. 191: "I had rather to adopt a
child," etc.

53. *How say you by,* etc. *By* here, as not unfrequently = *about*
or *concerning.* Cf. ii. 9. 24: "may be meant By the fool multitude." So Latimer (*Serm.*): "How think you by the ceremo-
nies," etc.

71. *Proper.* Comely, good-looking; as often. Cf. *Hebrews,* xi.
23: "a proper child," etc.

73. *Suited.* Dressed. Cf. "richly suited," *A. W.* i. 1. 170, etc.

Doublet. "The doublet (so called from being originally lined or wadded for defence) was a close-fitting coat, with skirts reaching a little below the girdle." The "round *hose*" were coverings for the legs, not the feet — "trowsers or breeches, reaching to the knee." The phrase "doublet and hose," as equivalent to "coat and breeches," occurs often in S. *Bonnet,* originally the name of a stuff, came to be applied to the man's cap made of it, as it still is in Scottish.

76. *The Scottish lord.* The *Scottish* of the quartos, printed before the accession of James I., was changed to *other* in the folio of 1623, to avoid giving offence to that monarch.

82. *Sealed under for another.* Became surety for another box on the ear. The whole passage is ironical. The Scotchman is too cowardly to return the blow, and the Frenchman offers to do it for him.

92. *You should refuse. Should* is often thus used by S. where we should use *would.* Cf. iii. 2. 267 below.

104. *Some other sort.* Some other way. *Imposition* = condition *imposed.* In iii. 4. 33 the word is used again in this literal sense of something "laid upon" one as a burden or duty.

106. *Sibylla.* Here used as a proper name, like "Sibyl" in *T. of S.* i. 2. 70. So Bacon, in *Colours of Good and Evil,* 10, speaks of "*Sybilla,* when she brought her three books." The reference here is to the Cumæan Sibyl, who, according to Ovid, obtained from Apollo a promise that her years should be as many as the grains of sand she was holding in her hand.

108. *This parcel of wooers.* Cf. "This youthful parcel of noble bachelors," *A. W.* ii. 3. 58.

123. *The four strangers.* There were six of them. Perhaps two were added after the first draft of the play ; or, quite as likely, it is another illustration of S.'s carelessness. See on i. 1. 177, 178.

127. *With so good heart as,* etc. We now seldom use *so . . . as,* preferring *as . . . as,* except where *so* requires special emphasis.

129. *Condition.* Nature, disposition. Cf. *Oth.* ii. 1. 255 : "she's full of most blessed condition." Cf. also "best conditioned," iii. 2. 288 below.

133. *Whiles.* The genitive singular of *while* (which was originally a noun) used as an adverb. It occurs in *Matthew,* v. 25.

SCENE III. — 1. *Ducats.* The value of the Venetian silver ducat was about that of the American dollar.

4. *For the which.* This archaism is occasionally found in S., as in the Bible (*Genesis,* i. 29, etc.).

7. *May you stead me?* Can you assist me? *May* originally expressed *ability,* as the noun *might* still does. *Can,* on the other hand, signified "to know or have skill." On *stead,* cf. *M. for M.* i. 4. 17 : "Can you so stead me As bring me to the sight of Isabella ?"

Pleasure me. So in *M. W.* i. 1. 251 : "What I do is to pleasure you, coz."

12. *A good man.* That is, "good" in the commercial sense — "having pecuniary ability ; of unimpaired credit."

17. *In supposition.* Doubtful, risked at sea.

18. *Tripolis.* The old name of *Tripoli,* a seaport of Syria, formerly of great commercial importance. Some take it to be the port of the same name in Barbary ; but this would seem to be disproved by the mention of both *Tripolis* and *Barbary* in iii. 2. 263, 264. The mention of *Mexico* in both passages is a slip noted by Karl Elze, as Venice does not appear to have had any trade with that country.

20. *Rialto.* The chief of the islands on which Venice was built. See p. 28 above. The name is from *rivo* (or *rio*) *alto,* deep stream ; not, as often stated, from *riva alta,* high bank. *Rivo alto* is sometimes wrongly translated as "high shore" or "high bank." Some editors also err in saying that the present bridge is not the one built in 1588–91. It took the place of an earlier wooden bridge, but has never been rebuilt.

21. *Squandered.* Scattered. So in Howell's *Letters*, 1650, we have "islands that lie squandered in the vast ocean." S. uses the word only here and in *A. Y. L.* ii. 7. 57: "squandering glances."

22. *There be land-rats.* In old English, besides the present tense *am*, etc., there was also this form *be*, from the Anglo-Saxon *beon*. The 2d pers. sing. was *beest*. The 1st and 3d pers. plu. *be* is often found in S. and the Bible.

32. *If it please you.* This impersonal form (cf. the French *s'il vous plait*), after being contracted into *if you please*, has come to be considered as personal, and we now say *if I please, if he pleases,* etc.

34. *Nazarite.* In the time of S. confounded with *Nazarene.* For *Nazarite* in the proper sense, see *Numbers*, vi.

36. *And so following.* And so forth. S. uses the phrase nowhere else.

41. *Publican.* Probably a tax-collector, not an innkeeper. Some critics consider *fawning* inconsistent with the former sense ; but the publicans, while arrogant to inferiors, might find it politic to fawn upon their superiors.

42. *For he is a Christian.* We should now say, *for being* a Christian. When thus used, *for* is often followed by *that,* as in the next line. Of course we could now say, "I hate him, for he is a Christian," but the meaning would be different. In this case, as in the other, the *for* is equivalent to *because,* but it connects more loosely, as the comma indicates. The difference in meaning is perhaps better illustrated by a case like the following (*M. for M.* ii. 1. 27) : —

> "You may not so extenuate his offence
> For I have had such faults ; "

that is, the fact that I have been guilty is no excuse for him. The modern reading would make nonsense of it.

46. *Upon the hip.* To "catch upon the hip" was a phrase used by wrestlers. Cf. iv. 1. 327 below, and *Oth.* ii. 1. 314.

51. *Which he calls interest.* Usance, usury, and *interest* were

equivalent terms in S.'s day. It was disreputable to take interest at all. It was considered " against nature for money to beget money." See Bacon's *Essay on Usurie*.

53. *Debating of my present store. Of* is often used by the Elizabethan writers in the sense of *about* or *concerning*. Cf. *Temp.* ii. 1. 81 : " You make me study of that," etc.

59. *Rest you fair.* God grant you good fortune ! *You* is the *object*, not the *subject*, of *rest.* Cf. "Rest you merry ! " (*R. and J.* i. 2. 65) and "God rest you merry ! " (*A. Y. L.* v. 1. 165).

62. *Excess.* More than the sum lent or borrowed; interest.

63. *Ripe wants.* Wants that admit of no delay, like ripe fruit that must be gathered at once.

64. *Possess'd.* Informed. Cf. iv. 1. 35 below: "I have possess'd your grace of what I purpose." The question is addressed to Bassanio.

65. *How much you would. Would* is often used absolutely, as here, for *wish* or *require*.

67. *I had forgot.* Of course this falsehood is part of Shylock's strategy. *You told me so* is said to Bassanio.

69. *Methought.* This *thought* is from the Anglo-Saxon verb *thyncan*, to seem, and not from *thencan*, to think. It is used impersonally, the *me* being a dative. *Methought* = it seemed to me.

71. *When Jacob*, etc. See *Genesis*, xxvii. and xxx.

74. *The third possessor.* Jacob may be included, as some suppose; but it is more likely that Shylock refers to Esau, who had been cheated of his heritage by the trickery of his " wise mother."

78. *Were compromis'd.* Had mutually agreed.

79. *Eanlings.* Lambs just brought forth; from Anglo-Saxon *eanian*, to bring forth. *Yeanling* is another form of the same word, and was substituted by Pope here.

Pied. Spotted. We have " daisies pied " in *L. L. L.* v. 2. 904 (and in Milton's *L'Allegro*); and in *Temp.* iii. 2. 71 Caliban calls Trinculo a " pied ninny," from the particoloured coat which he wore as a jester.

81. *Pill'd me.* Peeled. Cf. the Bible narrative (*Genesis*, xxx. 37, 38). The *me* is expletive, as often. See the dialogue between Petruchio and Grumio in *T. of S.* i. 2. 8 fol.

84. *Fall.* Let fall, bring forth.

90. *Was this inserted*, etc. Was this inserted in Scripture to justify usury?

94. *The devil can cite Scripture.* See *Matthew*, iv. 4, 6.

95. *Producing holy witness.* Adducing sacred authority.

101. *Beholding.* Often used by S., Bacon, and other writers of the time, instead of *beholden.*

102. *Many a time and oft.* An old phrase, still familiar. Here Shylock, perhaps irritated by Antonio's impatient question, which reminds him of the Merchant's arrogant and contemptuous treatment of him in the past, forgets for the moment the part he is playing; but Antonio's angry and scornful reply shows him the mistake he has made, and he at once resumes his artfully friendly tone.

107. *Misbeliever.* Strictly, one who believes *wrongly*, as *unbeliever* is one who does *not* believe, or an infidel. S. uses the word only here.

108. *Spet.* An obsolete spelling of *spit*, used occasionally by S., as it is by Milton in the one instance (*Comus*, 132) in which he employs the word.

Gaberdine. A long coarse frock. See *Temp.* ii. 2. 40, 115. The garment and the name are still used by the peasantry in some parts of England.

111. *Go to.* A phrase of exhortation or encouragement, sometimes used scornfully. Cf. *Temp.* v. 1. 297, etc.; also *Genesis*, xi. 4, etc.

130. *A breed of barren metal.* *Breed* is money *bred* from the principal. Shylock had used the same metaphor for interest. Cf. Middleton, *The Blacke Booke:* "coming to repay both the money and the breed of it — for interest may well be called the usurer's bastard," etc.

132. *Who if he break.* The "relative with a supplementary pronoun" often occurs in the writers of the time. Cf. *V. and A.* 935 : —

> " *Who*, when *he* liv'd, *his* breath and beauty set
>   Gloss on the rose, smell on the violet."

"If he *break*," that is, "break his day," fail to fulfil his engagement. Shylock uses the phrase in 159 below.

134. *I would be friends with you.* A "grammatical impropriety," but even now a familiar idiom.

136. *Doit.* A small Dutch coin, worth about a quarter of a cent.

141. *Your single bond.* Your individual bond, without sureties.
In a merry sport. In the old ballad of *Gernutus* (see page 24 above) the Jew says : —

> " But we will haue a merry iest,
>   for to be talked long :
> You shall make me a Band (quoth he)
>   that shall be large and strong.

> " And this shall be the forfeyture,
>   of your own Flesh a pound :
> If you agree, make you the Band,
>   and here is a hundred Crownes."

144. *Let the forfeit*, etc. Let the forfeit named be an exact (*equal*) pound of your flesh.

147. *Pleaseth me.* That is, "it pleaseth me" (the folio reading). See on 32 above.

151. *Dwell.* Continue, remain.

157. *Dealings teaches them suspect.* According to Abbott (*Grammar*, 333) and others, *teaches* is an instance of the old Northern plural in *es*, which is sometimes found in Elizabethan writers. They also sometimes omit the *to* of the infinitive (as here in *suspect*) after certain verbs which now require it, and sometimes insert it where now it is omitted.

163. *Muttons, beefs.* These Norman-French words are here used in their original sense. The plural *beeves* is still used for the living animals, and the singular form *beeve* is occasionally met with.

165. *If he will take it, so.* That is, *so be it,* or something of the kind. *So* was often thus used as a particle of assent or affirmation.

166. *For my love.* "For love's sake," as we say; or, perhaps, "as regards my love," or friendly feeling.

171. *Fearful guard Of an unthrifty knave. Fearful* = to be feared or *distrusted;* untrustworthy. *Knave,* which meant originally only a boy, and now means only a rogue, was in current use in S.'s time with either signification.

ACT II

SCENE I. — The stage direction in the first folio is: "*Enter Morochus a tawnie Moore all in white, and three or foure followers accordingly, with Portia, Nerrissa, and their traine. Flo. Cornets.*"

1. *Complexion.* A quadrisyllable. See on i. 1. 8 above.

6. *Let us make incision,* etc. Red blood was a traditionary sign of courage. Below (iii. 2. 86) Bassanio talks of cowards who "have livers white as milk."

7. *Reddest.* The use of the superlative in a comparison of two objects, though condemned by most of the modern grammars, is good old English.

8. *Aspect . . . fear'd.* On the accent of *aspect,* see on i. 1. 54 above. *Fear'd* = *caused* to fear, terrified. In *T. of S.* i. 2. 211 we have both senses of *fear* in close connection: "*Petruchio.* Tush! tush! fear boys with bugs. *Grumio.* For he fears none."

10. *Best-regarded.* Of highest estimation.

12. *To steal your thoughts.* To gain your love. *Thought* (both in the singular and the plural) not unfrequently refers to love in S., and *steal* is often associated with love, as suggesting its gradual and imperceptible development. Cf. v. 1. 19 below, for instance.

Note, by the way, that Morocco, though he may have come to Belmont as a fortune hunter, is honestly enamoured of the lady, as this entire speech, and all that he says, clearly prove. It is, indeed, his admiration and love for her that lead him to choose the wrong casket. Portia understands this, and, true woman that she is, shows it in her gentle, half-pitying treatment of him, though she is glad, of course, that he fails in the lottery.

14. *Nice direction.* Fastidious estimation.

17. *Scanted.* Limited, restricted. Cf. iii. 2. 112 below: "Scant this excess"; and v. 1. 141: "Scant this breathing courtesy."

18. *Wit.* In its original sense of *foresight, wisdom,* as in the familiar expressions, "at his wit's end," "lost his wits," etc.

20. *Yourself.* The pronouns *myself, thyself,* etc., were often used in S.'s time (as they still are in poetry) as the subject of a verb.

Stood as fair. Would have stood. In *fair* some suspect an allusion to the Moor's complexion, but this is not probable.

25. *The Sophy.* The *Sufi,* or Shah of Persia. Cf. *T. N.* ii. 5. 197, and iii. 4. 307. Bacon (*Essay* 43) speaks of "*Ismael,* the *Sophy* of *Persia.*"

26. *Sultan Solyman.* The most famous sultan of this name was Solyman the Magnificent, who reigned from 1520 to 1566.

31. *Alas the while !* This expression, like *Woe the while !* (*J. C.* i. 3. 82), seems originally to have meant, "Alas for the present state of things!" but it came to be used as indefinitely as the simple *alas !*

32. *Hercules and Lichas.* Lichas was the servant who brought to Hercules the poisoned tunic from Dejanira.

Play at dice Which is, etc. That is, in order to decide which is, etc. "The Elizabethan writers objected to scarcely any ellipsis, provided the deficiency could be easily supplied from the context."

35. *Alcides beaten by his page.* Alcides was the original name of Hercules, given him on account of his descent from Alcæus, the son of Perseus.

42. *Be advis'd.* Consider well, do not decide in haste. Cf. *advised* in i. 1. 142.

43. *Nor will not.* That is, will not "speak to lady," etc.

44. *The temple.* The chapel where the oath was to be taken.

46. *Blest or cursed'st.* *Blest* is an instance of the ellipsis of the superlative ending, not unusual at that time. Cf. *M. for M.* iv. 6. 13 : "The generous and gravest citizens." So Heywood: "Only the grave and wisest of the land; " and Ben Jonson: "The soft and sweetest music." In iii. 2. 288 we have "The best-conditioned and unwearied spirit," where the ellipsis is in the second adjective.

SCENE II. — The stage direction in the early eds. is " *Enter the clowne alone.*"

1. *Certainly my conscience will serve,* etc. This seems to express a hope rather than an assurance that this will be the result of the conflict between his conscience and the " fiend."

7. *As aforesaid.* From Launcelot's frequent use of legal phraseology we might infer that he had been in a lawyer's employ before he became the servant of Shylock; but the Jew, of course, was often engaged in litigation, and Launcelot may have picked up his law terms from that source.

9. *Scorn running with thy heels.* The play upon *heels* is obvious. Cf. *Much Ado,* iii. 4. 51 : "I scorn that with my heels."

10. *Via!* Away! (Italian). Cf. *M. W.* ii. 2. 159, *L. L. L.* v. 1. 156, etc.

11. *For the heavens!* Mason proposed to change *heavens* to *haven,* because " it is not likely that S. would make the *Devil* conjure Launcelot to do anything for *Heaven's sake ;* " but obviously the wit of the expression consists in that very incongruity.

19. *' Fiend,' say I, ' you counsel well.'* This is the folio reading; but some editors prefer that of the quarto, " counsel *ill.*" Launcelot probably says *well* because he prefers the fiend's advice.

21. *God bless* (or *save*) *the mark !* The origin and the meaning of this expression are alike obscure. It appears to be used most frequently " as a parenthetic apology for some profane or vulgar word."

25. *Incarnation.* For *incarnate*, of course.

31. *Enter old Gobbo.* The name is Italian for *hunchback*, and Steevens inferred that S. intended the character " to be represented with a hump back "; but the name was probably then a family one in Italy, as it is now. The Washington Hotel in Florence is now (1902) kept by a Gobbo, and I have seen the name in Pisa also. For the statue called *Il Gobbo di Rialto*, see p. 34 above. Tourists who have been in Verona will recollect another venerable *Il Gobbo* which sustains a holy-water basin in the church of Santa Anastasia.

34. *Sand-blind.* Dim of sight; as if there were sand in the eye, or perhaps floating before it. *High-gravel-blind* is Launcelot's own exaggeration of the word.

35. *Confusions.* A blunder for *conclusions*, which is the reading of one of the early quartos. To " try conclusions " (*Ham.* iii. 4. 195) was to try experiments.

41. *Marry.* A corruption of *Mary.* It was originally a mode of swearing by the Virgin, but its origin had come to be forgotten in S.'s day.

43. *God's sonties.* Corrupted from *God's saints*, or *sanctities*, or *santé* (health) — it is impossible to decide which.

50. *No master, sir*, etc. Furnivall quotes Sir Thomas Smith's *Commonwealth of England* (ed. 1612) : " As for gentlemen, they be made good cheap in England. For whosoeuer studieth the laws of the Realm, who studieth in the Uniuersities, who professeth liberall Sciences : and to be short, who can liue idely, and without manuall labour, and will beare the port, charge and countenance of a Gentleman, hee shall bee called *master*, for that is the tytle which men giue to Esquires, and other Gentlemen, and shall bee taken for a Gentleman."

52. *Well to live.* " With every prospect of a long life."

53. *What a' will.* *A'* for *he* is common in the old dramatists, in the mouths of peasants and illiterate people.

55. *Your worship's friend and Launcelot.* This has perplexed the critics. We might expect " *but* Launcelot " — from anybody

but Old Gobbo. He seems to mean, "He is your *friend*, and so you treat him as an equal and call him *Master*, but I call him plain *Launcelot.*"

57. *Talk you of young Master Launcelot?* The early eds. make this imperative, and not interrogative, and are followed by some editors, but the majority are clearly right in regarding it as a question. *Master* is emphatic.

60. *Father.* Launcelot twice calls Gobbo *father*, but the old man does not even suspect with whom he is talking, since the peasantry used to call all old people father or mother.

62. *The sisters three.* The Fates of classic fable.

87. *Your child that shall be.* Here some of the critics have been mystified by Launcelot's incongruous talk. Malone says, "Launcelot *probably* here indulges himself in talking nonsense," but he is not quite sure about it; and Steevens suggests that he "*may* mean that he shall hereafter prove his claim to the title of child by his dutiful behaviour," etc.

95. *Lord worshipped.* Perhaps, as some explain it = a lord worshipful, referring to the beard and the claim to the title of *Master ;* or *Lord worshipped may he be!* may be, as Mr. Gummere suggests, "merely another way of saying 'Lord be praised!'" According to stage tradition, Launcelot kneels with his back to the old man, who, "being sand-blind," mistakes the hair on his head for a beard.

97. *Fill-horse.* *Fill* for *thill*, or *shaft*, is a familiar word in New England, but in old England it is not known except as a provincialism in the Midland counties. We have "i' the fills" in *T. and C.* iii. 2. 48.

103. *Gree.* The spelling of all the early eds.

105. *I have set up my rest.* That is, I have determined. "A metaphor taken from play, where the highest stake the parties were disposed to venture was called the *rest.*" The expression occurs several times in the plays.

110. *Give me your present.* See on i. 3. 81 above.

122. *Gramercy*. A corruption of the French *grand merci*, "great thanks"; but it was often used as an expression of surprise, like "mercy on us!" as if derived from *grant mercy*.

132. *Cater-cousins*. The origin of the word is doubtful, but the meaning evidently is, that they do not seem much akin, or do not agree very well.

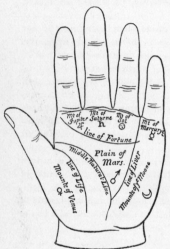

FROM A BOOK ON CHIROMANCY, 1558.

137. *A dish of doves.* See p. 31 above.

148. *Preferr'd thee.* To *prefer* often meant to "recommend for promotion," and sometimes to "promote."

151. *The old proverb.* Alluding to the Scotch proverb, "The grace of God is gear enough."

157. *Guarded.* Trimmed, ornamented. The broidered edging *guarded* (protected) the cloth from wear. See *Hen. VIII.* prol. 16 and *Much Ado*, i. 1. 288.

158. *In.* Go in; as in *C. of E.* v. 1. 37, etc.

159. *Well, if any man*, etc. The construction is, "Well, if any man in Italy which doth offer to swear upon a book have a fairer table" — the expression being like "any man that breathes," etc. After having thus admired his table, he breaks off to predict his good fortune. As Johnson remarks, "the act of expanding his hand" reminds him of laying it on the book in taking an oath.

In chiromancy, or palmistry, the *table line*, or *line of fortune*, is the one running from the forefinger below the other fingers to the side of the hand. The *natural line* is the one running through the middle of the palm. The *line of life* is the one which encircles the ball of the thumb. The space between the two first is called *mensa,* or the *table.*

163. *Aleven.* A vulgarism for *eleven.*

168. *For this gear.* See on i. 1. 110 above.

172. *Bestow'd.* Put away, disposed of. Cf. 2 *Kings,* v. 24, etc. See also *J. C.* i. 3. 151, etc.

182. *Hear thee.* In this, as in some other expressions ("fare thee well," etc.), *thee* appears to be used for *thou,* and not reflexively.

187. *Liberal.* Free, reckless; but not in so bad a sense as in *Much Ado,* iv. i. 93 ("a liberal villain"), where it means licentious.

Take pain. We now use only the plural, "take pains." S. uses both. See below, v. 1. 180.

189. *Thy skipping spirit.* Thy frolicsome humour. Cf. *Ham.* iii. 4. 123: "Upon the heat and flame of thy distemper Sprinkle cool patience." *Spirit* is often a monosyllable, as if pronounced *sprit* (not *sprite*).

198. *Studied in a sad ostent.* Trained to put on a sober aspect. Below (ii. 8. 44) we have "fair ostents (manifestations, tokens) of love."

207. *I must to Lorenzo.* This ellipsis of the verb was common, especially after *will;* as "I 'll to him," *R. and J.* iii. 2. 141, etc.

SCENE III. — 10. *Exhibit.* For *inhibit* (restrain).

15. *What heinous sin.* Possibly this is one of the instances in which *what* is used for *what a.* Cf. *J. C.* i. 3. 42: "What night is this!" But *sin* may be used in the general sense of *sinfulness.*

SCENE IV. — 5. *We have not spoke us yet of.* We have not yet bespoken.

6. *Quaintly.* Tastefully, gracefully. *Quaint* in the old writers means *elegant,* and hence *artful, ingenious.* In Johnson's day it had come to mean *affected,* and now it has "the united sense of *antique* and *odd.*" Cf. "quaint lies" below, iii. 4. 69.

7. *Not undertook.* We have "underta'en" in *W. T.* iii. 2. 79, and "to be undertook" in *Oth.* v. 2. 311. S. often uses two or more forms of the participle. Thus in *J. C.* we have *stricken, struck,* and *strucken.* So we find *mistook* and *mistaken,* etc. We must bear in mind that the Elizabethan age was a transitional period in the history of the language.

10. *Break up.* Break open. *Break up* was a term in carving; and in *L. L. L.* iv. 1. 56 we have "break up this capon," where the "capon" is a letter.

13. *Writ.* S. uses both *writ* and *wrote* for the past tense, and *writ, written,* and *wrote* for the participle.

23. *Provided of. Of* is often used of the agent (where we use *by*), and of the instrument (for *with*), as here. Cf. *Macb.* i. 2. 13: "supplied of kernes," etc.

26. *Some hour.* About an hour; as we say *some two hours, some six months ago,* etc.

29. *Needs.* Of necessity; a genitive used adverbially.

Directed . . . What gold, etc. The ellipsis here is very like what is called a *zeugma.*

35. *Dare.* Either the "subjunctive used imperatively" or the 3d pers. of the imperative.

37. *Faithless.* Unbelieving; as in *Matthew,* xvii. 17.

SCENE V. — 2. *Difference of.* Cf. *Lear,* iv. 2. 26: "O, the difference of man and man!" See also iv. 1. 361 below.

3. *What, Jessica!* A customary exclamation of impatience, in calling to persons; like *when* (*Temp.* i. 2. 316, *J. C.* ii. 1. 5, etc.).

11. *Bid forth.* Invited out. Cf. "find forth," i. 1. 143 above, and "feasting forth," 37 below. S. uses *bidden* only in *Much Ado,* iii. 3. 32. He uses both *bade* and *bid* for the past tense. See on ii. 5. 7 above.

17. *Towards my rest.* Against my peace of mind. To dream of money was supposed to be unlucky.

18. *To-night.* That is, last night; as in *J. C.* iii. 3. 1: "I

dream'd to-night that I did feast with Cæsar." Usually in S. it has its modern meaning.

21. *So do I his.* Shylock plays upon Launcelot's blunder of *reproach* for *approach.*

25. *Black-Monday.* Easter Monday; so called, as the old chronicler Stowe tells us, because "in the 34th of Edward III. (1360), the 14th of April, and the morrow after Easter-day, King Edward with his host lay before the city of Paris: which day was full dark of mist and hail, and so bitter cold that many men died on their horses' backs with the cold."

30. *The wry-neck'd fife. Wry-necked* may refer to the fife or to the fifer, but the former is more probable, on account of the preceding *drum.* Barnaby Rich (1618) says: "A fife is a wry-neckt musician, for he always looks away from his instrument." On the other hand, the old English fife (like one used in classical times) had a bent mouthpiece. It was called the *flute à bec,* as the mouthpiece resembled the beak of a bird.

36. *Jacob's staff.* See *Genesis,* xxxii. 10, and *Hebrews,* xi. 21. In Spenser, *F. Q.* i. 6. 35, "Iacobs staffe" more probably refers to St. James (Jacobus), who is usually represented with a pilgrim's hat and staff.

37. *Of feasting forth. Of = for,* as often. See on 11 above.

43. *Jewess' eye.* It is "Jewes" in the quartos and 1st and 2d folios, "Jew's" in the later folios. Pope suggested *Jewess',* which has been generally adopted. Launcelot's phrase is a slight alteration of the proverbial expression, *Worth a Jew's eye.* The Jews were often threatened with the loss of an eye, or some other mutilation, in order to extort treasure from them.

46. *Patch.* A name given to the professional jester (from his patched or particoloured coat), and afterwards used as a term of contempt.

52. *Perhaps I will return.* The shade of meaning is such as would now be expressed by *will* — "Perhaps I may decide to return," or something of the sort. "I *shall* return" would be future

pure and simple; "I *will* return" *adds* the idea that the possible
future act depends upon the speaker's *will.*

SCENE VI. — 5. *Venus' pigeons.* The chariot of Venus was
drawn by doves. In *Temp.* iv. 1. 94 she is described as "dove-
drawn," and her "doves" are also referred to in *M. N. D.* i. 1. 171,
etc.

7. *Obliged.* Pledged, plighted.

9. *Sits down.* That is, sits down *with.* So in the next sentence,
"pace them (with)." This ellipsis of a preposition which has
already been expressed *before* the relative is quite common in S.
Cf. below (iv. 1. 382): "A gift of all (of which) he dies possess'd."
See also on i. 1. 125 above.

10. *Untread again.* Retrace.

14. *Younger.* The reading of all the early eds., changed by
some to *younker,* which S. uses in 1 *Hen. IV.* iii. 3. 92 and 3 *Hen.
VI.* ii. 1. 24.

15. *Scarfed.* Decked with flags and streamers. In *A. W.* ii. 3.
214 "scarfs" are associated with "bannerets" in the comparison
of a person to a "vessel."

17. *How like the prodigal doth she return.* The reference to the
Scripture parable is obvious. The *she* is naturally used of the *bark.*

18. *Over-weather'd.* Weatherbeaten.

30. *Who love I,* etc. The inflection of *who* is often neglected.
Directly after a preposition, *whom* is usually found. Cf. *L. L. L.* ii.
1. 2: "Consider *who* the king your father sends, To *whom* he
sends." But in *Cymb.* iv. 2. 75 and *Oth.* i. 2. 52 we have the interrogative *who* even after a preposition: "To *who?*" See on i. 2.
32 above. Sweet, in his *Short Historical English Grammar* (Oxford, 1892), says: "In present spoken English *whom* may be said
to be extinct, except in the rare construction with a preposition
immediately before it."

35. *Exchange.* That is, of apparel.

42. *Too-too light.* "Too-too" was often (as here) a compound

epithet, and should then have the hyphen; but in some cases (as in *Ham.* i. 2. 129: "this too, too solid flesh") it was an emphatic repetition, just as it is now.

43. *An office of discovery*, etc. The office of a torchbearer is to show what is in the way, but I ought to keep in the shade.

47. *Close.* Secret, stealthy.

51. *By my hood.* Probably swearing by the *hood* of his masque dress. In *Gentile* there is perhaps a play upon *gentle*, which is found in some of the early eds.

52. *Beshrew me.* A very mild imprecation, often used playfully and even tenderly.

54. *If that.* This use of *that* as "a conjunctional affix" was common. Thus we have "when that," "why that," "while that," "though that," "since that," etc.

67. *Glad on 't.* S. often uses *on* where we should use *of.* In *Temp.* i. 2, *on 't = of it* occurs three times. See also 1 *Samuel*, xxvii. 11.

SCENE VII. — 4. *Of gold, who.* In the Elizabethan age, *which* was not yet established as the neuter relative. It was often applied to persons (as in the Lord's Prayer, "Our Father *which* art in heaven") and *who* to things. In the next line but one, we have "silver, *which*."

5. *Who chooseth*, etc. The inscriptions are all in Alexandrines (verses of six accents or twelve syllables).

26. *If thou be'st rated.* This *beest* must not be confounded with the subjunctive *be.* It is the Anglo-Saxon *bist*, 2d pers. sing. pres. indicative of *beón*, to be. See on i. 3. 22 above.

29. *Afeard.* S. uses *afeard* and *afraid* interchangeably.

30. *Disabling.* Disparaging; as in *A. Y. L.* iv. 1. 34. v. 4. 80, etc.

34. *But more than these, in love I do deserve.* This line alone would prove that Morocco is really in love. See on ii. 1. 12 above.

41. *Hyrcanian.* Hyrcania was an extensive tract of country

southeast of the Caspian. S. three times mentions the tigers of Hyrcania: 3 *Hen. VI.* i. 4. 155, *Macb.* iii. 4. 101, and *Ham.* ii. 2. 472. *Vasty* = waste, desolate, like the Latin *vastus*. S. uses *vast* several times as a noun = *waste*.

42. *Throughfares. Thorough* and *through* are the same word, and S. uses either as suits the measure. So with *throughly* and *thoroughly*. We find *throughfare* again in *Cymb.* i. 2. 11.

43. *Come view.* Come to view. See on i. 3. 157 above.

49. *Like.* Likely; as very often.

GOLDEN ANGEL OF QUEEN ELIZABETH

50. *Too gross*, etc. Too coarse a material to enclose her shroud. *Cerecloth* = *cerement* (*Ham.* i. 4. 48), cloth smeared with melted wax (Lat. *cera*) or gums, for embalming the dead.

51. *Obscure* has the accent on the first syllable, like many dissyllabic adjectives and participles when used before a noun.

53. *Undervalued*, etc. See on i. 1. 165 above. During the Middle Ages, and down to the sixteenth century, the value of silver was $\frac{1}{12}$ and $\frac{1}{11}$, and even, as here stated, $\frac{1}{10}$ that of gold. In the latter part of the seventeenth century it fell to as low as $\frac{1}{16}$. In the eighteenth it rose to $\frac{1}{14}$, and is now $\frac{1}{18}$ or less.

57. *Insculp'd upon.* Graven on the outside. The *angel* was worth about ten shillings. It had on one side a figure of Michael piercing the dragon. The use of the device is said to have origi-

nated in Pope Gregory's pun of *Angli* and *Angeli*. Verstegan, in his *Restitution of Decayed Intelligence*, says: "The name of *Engel* is yet at this present in all the Teutonick tongues, to wit, the high and low Dutch, &c., as much to say as Angel, and if a Dutch-man be asked how he would in his language call an Angel-like-man, he would answer, *ein English-man*, *Engel* being in their tongue an Angel, and English, which they write *Engelsche*, Angel-like. And such reason and consideration may have moved our former kings, upon their best coin of pure and fine gold, to set the image of an angel."

63. *A carrion death.* That is, a skull.

65. *Glisters.* *Glisten* does not occur in S. nor in Milton. In both we find *glister* several times.

77. *Part.* Depart. See *Cor.* v. 6. 73: "When I parted hence," etc. *Depart* was also used where we should say *part;* as in the Marriage Service, "till death us do part" is a corruption of "till death us depart."

Scene VIII. — 12. *A passion.* Passionate outcry. Cf. *T. and C.* v. 2. 181 : "Your passion draws ears hither."

27. *Reason'd.* Talked, conversed; as in *Rich. III.* ii. 3. 39, etc.

28. *The narrow seas.* The English Channel — a name not unfrequently applied to it in that day. It occurs again iii. 1. 4 below.

30. *Fraught.* We now use *fraught* (= *freighted*) only in a figurative sense. *Fraught* is used as a noun in *T. N.* v. 1. 64 and *Oth.* iii. 3. 449. *Freight* does not occur in S. or Milton.

33. *You were best.* Originally the *you* was dative (*to* you it were best), but it came to be regarded as a nominative. Cf. *J. C.* iii. 3. 13 : "Ay, and truly, you were best;" *Temp.* i. 2. 366 : "Thou'rt best;" *T. N.* i. 2. 27 : "She were better," etc. See also v. 1. 175 below.

39. *Slubber.* To do carelessly or imperfectly. It also means to obscure, or soil; as in *Oth.* i. 3. 227 : "slubber the gloss of your new fortunes."

40. *Riping*. Ripeness, maturity.

42. *Mind of love*. That is, loving mind. Cf. "mind of honour," *M. for M*. ii. 4. 179.

44. *Ostents*. Manifestations, displays. See on ii. 2. 198 above.

45. *Conveniently*. In its original sense, fitly, suitably. Cf. the adjective in iii. 4. 56 below.

47. *Turning his face*, etc. As Malone suggests, we have here "the outline of a beautiful picture."

48. *Sensible*. Sensitive. Cf. *L. L. L*. iv. 3. 337: "Love's feeling is more soft and sensible Than are the tender horns of cockled snails."

52. *Quicken his embraced heaviness*. Enliven the melancholy he indulges. Cf. iii. 2. 109 below: "rash-embrac'd despair."

53. *Do we so*. 1st pers. imperative (or "subjunctive used imperatively"); a form not uncommon in S. Cf. *Hen. V*. iv. 8. 127: "Do we all holy rites!" See also v. 1. 36 below.

SCENE IX. — 18. *Address'd me*. Prepared myself.

Fortune now, etc. Success now to the hope of my heart!

25. *By the fool multitude*. For *by*, see on i. 2. 53; and for the adjective *fool*, on i. 1. 102 above.

26. *Fond*. Foolish; as usually in S. Cf. iii. 3. 9 below.

27. *The martlet*. The house-martin. Cf. *Macb*. i. 6. 4: "the temple-haunting martlet."

28. *In the weather*. Exposed to the weather. Cf. *Cymb*. iii. 3. 64: "left me bare to weather."

31. *Jump with*. Agree with. Cf. *Rich. III*. iii. 1. 11: "outward show, which . . . seldom or never jumpeth with the heart." *Jump* also means to risk, hazard, as in *Macb*. i. 7. 7: "jump the life to come."

40. *Estates*. Ranks. Cf. *Ham*. v. 1. 244: "'t was of some estate" (that is, high rank).

43. *Should cover*, etc. Should wear their hats, that now take them off, as to superiors.

47. *Ruin.* Refuse, rubbish.

52. *Too long a pause*, etc. This is perhaps an *Aside*, as Capell and Furness assume, but I doubt it.

60. *To offend*, etc. That is, an offender cannot be the judge of his own case. For the accent of *distinct*, see on ii. 7. 51 above.

62. *Fire.* As often, a dissyllable. In *J. C.* iii. 1. 171 we have it both as a monosyllable and as a dissyllable: "As fire drives out fire, so pity pity." *Hours* is a dissyllable four times in as many lines in 3 *Hen. VI.* ii. 5. 31–34, and a monosyllable four lines below. Cf. iii. 2. 20 below.

67. *I wis.* This is a corruption of the adverbial *ywis* (certainly), but S. no doubt regarded it as a pronoun and verb.

71. *You are sped.* Your fate is settled. Cf. "you two are sped," *T. of S.* v. 2. 185. See also *Lycidas*, 122: "What need they? They are sped."

77. *Wroth.* Some make the word = *ruth* (sorrow); but others take it to be another form of *wrath*, used in the old sense of misfortune or calamity.

84. *My lord.* Used jestingly in response to the *my lady*. So in 1 *Hen. IV.* ii. 4. 317 the prince says, "How now, my lady the hostess?" in reply to her "My lord the Prince!" In *Rich. II.* v. 5. 67, also, a groom addresses the king, "Hail, royal prince!" and Richard replies, "Thanks, noble peer!"

88. *Sensible regreets.* Tangible greetings, substantial salutations. *Regreet* strictly means a responsive greeting. The noun occurs again in *K. John*, iii. 1. 241.

89. *Commends.* Cf. *Rich. II.* iii. 1. 38: "I send to her my kind commends."

90. *Yet I have not.* I have not yet. *Yet* = up to this time, is now used only *after* a negative, but in the Elizabethan age it was often used, as here, *before* a negative. Cf. *T. of S.* ind. 1. 96: "For yet his honour never heard a play;" and this from Ascham's *Scholemaster:* "There be that kepe them out of fier and yet was never burned" — which would be nonsense nowadays.

91. *Likely.* In the Yankee sense of *promising.* Cf. 2 *Hen. IV.* iii. 2. 186: "a likely fellow!" and *Id.* iii. 2. 273: "your likeliest men."

97. *High-day wit.* "Holiday terms," as Hotspur expresses it (1 *Hen. IV.* i. 3. 46). Cf. *M. W.* iii. 2. 60: "he speaks holiday."

99. *Cupid's post.* So below (v. 1. 46) we have "there's a post come from my master." For the adverbial *mannerly,* cf. *Cymb.* iii. 6. 92, etc.

100. *Bassanio, lord Love,* etc. May it be Bassanio, O Cupid!

ACT III

SCENE I. — 2. *It lives there unchecked.* The report prevails there uncontradicted.

3. *Wracked.* The only spelling of *wrecked* in the early eds. The noun *wrack* (never *wreck*) rhymes with *back* in *Macb.* v. 5. 51 and four other instances in S.

4. *The Goodwins.* The Goodwin Sands, off the eastern coast of Kent. According to tradition, they were once an island belonging to Earl Godwin, which was swallowed up by the sea about A.D. 1100.

9. *Knapped.* Nibbled; originally, snapped, broke off. The word occurs in *Psalms,* xlvi. 9 (Prayer-Book version): "He knappeth the spear in sunder." *Ginger* was a favourite condiment with old people.

27. *The wings,* etc. The boy's clothes she wore when she eloped.

37. *Match.* Bargain, compact. Cf. *Cymb.* iii. 6. 30: "'t is our match," etc.

39. *Smug.* Spruce, trim. Cf. *Lear,* iv. 6. 202: "a smug bridegroom."

48. *Half a million.* That is, ducats.

62. *Humility.* The word is used in its ordinary sense, but is spoken ironically: "What is his professed *humility?*" — the humility, or patience under injuries inculcated by his "prophet the

Nazarite " (in *Matthew*, v. 39, for instance). It has essentially the same meaning as *sufferance*, which Shylock here opposes to it: If the *humility* of the Christian is *revenge*, what should the *sufferance* of the Jew be "by Christian example"? Schmidt defines it in this and a few other passages as "kindness, benevolence, humanity," and some critics have been inclined to agree with him;

THE GOODWIN SANDS, DURING A STORM

but in all these passages the ordinary sense of the word is equally or more satisfactory. The *New English Dictionary* (Oxford) does not recognize "humanity" among the meanings of *humility*, which it illustrates by abundant examples from the fourteenth to the nineteenth century.

65. *It shall go hard*, etc. I will spare no effort to outdo you in what you teach me.

71. *Matched.* That is, matched with them, found to match them.

85. *Why, so.* Well, well. Cf. *Rich. II.* ii. 2. 87, etc.

115. *My turquoise.* The folio reads, "my Turkies." Tennyson spells it *turkis*, which is still an allowed pronunciation. Marvellous properties were ascribed to this "Turkey-stone." Its colour was said to change with the health of the wearer. Cf. Ben Jonson, *Sejanus* : —

> " And true as Turkise in the deare lord's ring,
> Looke well or ill with him."

And Fenton (*Secret Wonders of Nature*, 1569) says: "The *Turkeys* doth move when there is any perill prepared to him that weareth it."

SCENE II. — 6. *Hate counsels not*, etc. Hatred would prompt no such feeling.

8. *And yet a maiden hath no tongue but thought.* And yet a maiden must not venture to speak all that she feels; or, if she speak at all, she must speak what she feels. The line has been much discussed. See more than a full page in fine print upon it in Furness's "New Variorum" ed.

14. *Beshrew.* See on ii. 6. 52 above.

15. *O'erlook'd.* Bewitched by the "evil eye." Cf. *M. W.* v. 5. 87 : "thou wast o'erlook'd even in thy birth."

18. *Naughty.* Evil. See on iii. 3. 9 below.

20. *Though yours, not yours.* One *yours* (preferably the second) must be a dissyllable. See on ii. 9. 62 above.

Prove it so, etc. If it prove so (that is, that I am "not yours "), let fortune, not me, bear the penalty. See on 314 below.

22. *Peize.* The French *peser*, to weigh. Here it means to delay, as if weighing each moment deliberately, or (as some explain the figure) as if the time were retarded by hanging weights to it. S. uses the word in the sense of *weigh* in *Rich. II.* v. 3. 105, and in that of *poise* in *K. John*, ii. 1. 575.

26. *Then confess*, etc. Alluding to the use of the rack to extort confession.

29. *Fear the enjoying.* Fear *for* the enjoying. Cf. iii. 5. 3 and 29 below.

44. *A swan-like ena.* Cf. *Oth.* v. 2. 247: "I will play the swan, And die in music"; and *K. John*, v. 7. 21: "this pale, faint swan, Who chants a doleful hymn to his own death."

54. *Presence.* Dignity of mien.

55. *Alcides.* Laomedon, king of Troy, had offended Neptune, who threatened to inundate the country unless the monarch should sacrifice his daughter Hesione. Accordingly, she was fastened to a rock on the seashore to become the prey of a sea monster. Hercules rescued her, not for "love," but to get possession of a pair of famous horses belonging to the king.

58. *Dardanian wives.* Trojan women. Cf. *Hen. V.* iii. 3. 40, etc.

63. *Fancy.* Love; as often. Cf. *M. N. D.* i. 1. 155: "sighs and tears, poor fancy's followers." So also in compounds, as "fancy-free" (*M. N. D.* ii. 1. 164), "fancy-sick" (*Id.* iii. 2. 96), etc. The *Song* describes in exquisite imagery the birth and the death of a transient affection, "engendered in the eye," not in the heart.

74. *Still.* Ever. See on i. 1. 17 above.

76. *Season'd.* This carries on the metaphor suggested by *tainted.* It is a homely figure, taken from the use of salt to preserve meat, but it is a favourite one with S.

79. *Approve.* Justify, prove.

81. *No vice so simple.* So unmixed.

82. *His outward parts.* Its outward parts. *Its* was just coming into use in the Elizabethan age. It does not occur in the present play, or in any earlier one, except once in 2 *Hen. VI.* iii. 2. 393, where the folio has *it's* and the old play has *his.* In the folio the form *its* is found only in *M. for M.* i. 2. 4, while *it's* occurs nine times. *It* as a genitive (or "possessive") is found fourteen times, in seven of which it precedes *own.* This *it* is an early provincial form of the old genitive. In King James's version of the Bible

(1611) *its* does not occur at all, and the possessive *it* only in *Leviticus*, xxv. 5 ("it own accord"), changed in modern editions to "its own."

86. *Livers white as milk.* See on ii. 1. 6 above.

87. *Excrement.* Used, as the related word *excrescence* still is, for a superficial growth. It refers here to the *beards;* as in *L. L. L.* v. 1. 109: "dally with my excrement, with my mustachio." It is also applied to the hair in *C. of E.* ii. 2. 79 and *W. T.* iv. 4. 734.

91. *Lightest.* That is, in a bad sense. Cf. below (v. 1. 129), "Let me give light, but let me not be light," etc.

92. *Crisped.* Curled. Milton (*Comus*, 984) speaks of "crisped shades and bowers," referring to the leaves waved and curled by the wind.

94. *Upon supposed fairness.* On the strength of their fictitious beauty. The expression seems to be closely connected with the preceding line, and not with the one before that, as some make it.

95. *The dowry*, etc. S. has several times expressed his antipathy to false hair. In *Sonn.* 68 there is a passage very similar to the one in the text. See also *T. of A.* iv. 3. 144: "Thatch your poor thin roofs With burdens of the dead." In *L. L. L.* iv. 3. 258 Biron says : —

> "O, if in black my lady's brows be deck'd,
>   It mourns that painting and usurping hair
>   Should ravish doters with a false aspect."

It was then comparatively a recent fashion. Stow says, "Women's periwigs were first brought into England about the time of the massacre of Paris" (1572). Barnaby Rich, in 1615, says of the periwig sellers : "These attire-makers within these forty years were not known by that name. . . . But now they are not ashamed to set them forth upon their stalls — such monstrous mop-poles of hair — so proportioned and deformed that but within these twenty or thirty years would have drawn the passers-by to stand and gaze, and to wonder at them."

97. *Guiled.* Full of guile, treacherous. S. has many similar

participial adjectives derived from nouns, and meaning "endowed
with (the noun)."

99. *An Indian beauty.* This has been a great stumbling-block
to the critics, who have proposed "dowdy," "gipsy," "favour"
(= face), "visage," "feature," "beldam," etc., in place of *beauty.*
Indian is used in a derogatory sense, and the occurrence of *beauteous* and *beauty* in the same sentence is not at all unlike S.'s
manner.

102. *Hard food for Midas.* An allusion to the story of Midas,
king of Phrygia, who gained from Bacchus the power to change
whatever he touched to gold, and found to his sorrow that even his
food was thus transmuted.

I will none of thee. See on ii. 2. 207 above.

106. *Thy plainness.* The folio and both quartos have "pale-
nesse." Warburton suggested the emendation, which is adopted
by the majority of editors. The antithesis of *plainness* and *eloquence* is more natural and more forcible, especially after that of
threatenest and *promise* in the preceding line. It is an objection to
paleness that *pale* has just been applied to the *silver* casket.

110. *Green-eyed jealousy.* Cf. "green-eyed monster," in *Oth.* iii.
3. 166.

112. *Rain thy joy.* The later quartos have *rein*, which some
prefer; but *in measure* expresses the idea of restraint, so that *In
measure rain thy joy* corresponds to both *allay thy ecstasy* and
scant this excess. The succession of antitheses emphasizes the
idea. *In measure rein* would introduce a weak tautology.

115. *Counterfeit.* Portrait. Cf. *T. of A.* v. 1. 83: "Thou
draw'st a counterfeit Best in all Athens."

120. *Hairs.* Cf. *L. L. L.* iv. 3. 142: "her hairs were gold," etc.

126. *Unfurnish'd.* Unaccompanied by the other eye, or, perhaps, by the other features.

130. *Continent.* In its original sense of *that which contains.*
Cf. *Ham.* iv. 4. 64: "tomb enough and continent"; and v. 2. 115:
"you shall find in him the continent of what part a gentleman

would see " (that is, find him containing every quality which a gentleman would desire to contemplate for imitation).

140. *I come by note*, etc. " I come according to written warrant
(the scroll just read) to give a kiss and receive the lady."

141. *Prize.* By metonymy, for the contest.

156. *Livings.* Possessions, fortune. Cf. v. 1. 260: "you have
given me life and living." See also *Mark*, xii. 44, etc.

158. *Sum of nothing.* This is the reading of the folio, and is
more in keeping with the negative characteristics which follow than
" sum of something," the reading of the quartos, which some editors adopt. *To term in gross* = to state in full; to make the
most of it. Cf. *gross* in i. 3. 55 above.

174. *Be my vantage*, etc. Be a sufficient ground for my crying
out against you. "Exclaim *on*" occurs elsewhere, but S. also uses
" exclaim against."

178. *Fairly spoke.* S. uses both *spoke* and *spoken* as participles.
See on ii. 4. 7 above.

191. *None from me.* That is, none *away* from me, since you
have enough yourselves. This meaning of *from* is not uncommon,
and is played upon in *Rich. III.* iv. 4. 256–261.

195. *So thou canst get.* If thou canst; a common use of *so*.

197. *As swift.* The Elizabethan writers use adjectives freely as
adverbs.

199. *Intermission.* Delay; that is, I can be as prompt in
making love as you are. Some editors follow the 1st folio, which
joins *intermission* to *lov'd*. The meaning then is, I made love for
pastime, or to occupy myself while you were wooing Portia. *Intermission* is metrically five syllables. See on i. 1. 8 above.

208. *Achiev'd her mistress.* S. often uses *achieve* in this sense.
Cf. *T. of S.* i. 1. 161 : " If I achieve not this young modest girl," etc.

212. *Our feast shall be.* *Shall* = *will*, as often. See on i. 1. 117
above.

214. *Salerio.* Some critics have doubted whether this is the
name of a new character, or one of the various forms of *Salarino*

or *Salanio* found in the old editions ; but that it is the former is probable from the fact that the name is spelt *Salerio* in *every instance* in which it occurs (five times in the text and once in a stage direction) in both the quartos and the folios, while *Salarino* and *Salanio* appear as *Salarino, Salaryno, Salerino, Slarino, Solarino, Solanio, Salino, Salinio,* and *Solania.* Furness thinks that the limited number of actors in the old theatres would prevent the introduction of a new character here ; but this play has fewer characters than the average, even if we add Salerio.

216. *If that.* See on ii. 6. 54 above.

218. *Very friends.* True friends. Cf. *R. and J.* iii. 1. 115: " My very friend." See also *John,* vii. 26.

228. *Doth. Dost* and *doth* are the established forms for the auxiliary; *doest* and *doeth*, in other cases. In old writers we find the former used for the latter, as here. Cf. *J. C.* i. 1. 8: " What dost thou with thy best apparel on ? "

231. *Estate.* State, condition ; as often. On the other hand, *state* is sometimes found in the sense of *estate.* See 254 below.

235. *Success.* Elsewhere S. often uses this word in its old sense of *issue, result.*

236. *Won the fleece.* Cf. i. 1. 170 above.

238. *Shrewd.* Evil; the original sense of the word.

239. *Steals.* A relative in S. often takes a singular verb though the antecedent be plural.

242. *Constant.* Steadfast, self-possessed. Cf. *Temp.* i. 2. 207: " Who was so firm, so constant," etc.

246. *Unpleasant'st.* This harsh contraction of superlatives was common. Cf. *Macb.* ii. 1. 24: " At your kind'st leisure "; *Id.* ii. 2. 4: " stern'st good night," etc.

257. *Mere.* Absolute, thorough. Cf. *Oth.* ii. 2. 3: " The mere perdition of the Turkish fleet," etc.

261. *Issuing.* Pouring forth. Intransitive verbs are not unfrequently used transitively by S.

262. *Hit.* Hit the mark, succeeded.

265. *Scape.* Not to be printed " 'scape." It is found often in prose.

267. *Should appear.* Would appear. See on i. 2. 92.

268. *Discharge.* Pay. Cf. *C. of E.* iv. 4. 122: "I will discharge thee."

271. *Confound.* Destroy, ruin; as often.

273. *Impeach the freedom of the state.* Denies that strangers have equal rights in Venice. Cf., however, iv. 1. 38, where Shylock says: —

> " If you deny me, let the danger light
> Upon your charter and your city's freedom ; "

as if the freedom depended upon a charter which might be revoked by the power that had granted it. The thought here may be the same.

275. *Magnificoes of greatest port.* Grandees of highest rank.

276. *Persuaded with.* Used persuasion with. It is the only instance in which S. joins *with* to this verb.

277. *Envious.* Malicious. So *envy* = malice, in iv. 1. 10, 121 below; as often.

280. *To Tubal and to Chus.* Karl Elze says that the names are "taken from *Genesis*, x. 2, 6, without change "; but there the latter name is *Cush.* Perhaps *Chus* in the old eds. was a misprint for *Cush.* According to the dictionaries, *ch* is pronounced like *k* in all Hebrew proper names, with the single exception of *Rachel;* but *Chus,* if it be a true Hebrew name, should probably be regarded as another exception.

284. *Deny.* Forbid. Elsewhere it means *refuse ;* as in ii. 2. 180, etc.

288. *Best-condition'd and unwearied.* That is, *most unwearied.* See on ii. 1. 46 above. For *conditioned,* see on i. 2. 129 above.

296. *Description.* A quadrisyllable. See on 199 above.

297. *Hair.* A dissyllable. See on ii. 9. 62 above.

307. *Cheer.* In its original meaning of *countenance.* Cf. *M. N. D.* iii. 2. 96 : " pale of cheer," etc. It is the French *chère*, which even

up to the sixteenth century was used in the sense of *head, face.* In some of the provincial dialects of France the word still retains its old meaning.

308. *Dear bought.* "Dearly bought" (iv. 1. 95); the adjective used adverbially, as often.

One would suppose that the playfulness of this line, with its pretty pun on *dear*, was self-evident, but some critics take it in all seriousness. One, for instance, says : "Portia could not possibly intend by these words ungenerously to remind Bassanio of the benefits she had conferred upon him. They must, I think, relate to that anxiety and distress of mind which she had undergone during the time that his fate was in suspense ; possibly, too, to the grief she was now about to suffer in his absence." In other words, Portia does not refer to her marriage with Bassanio as a mercantile transaction, but she does remind him that she has had to pay a rather heavy price for him in mental anxiety on his behalf.

312. *Is forfeit.* Is forfeited. So below, iv. 1. 358: "thy wealth being forfeit." This contraction is not uncommon in the past participle of verbs ending in *-ed* or *-t.* See on v. 1. 11 below.

314. *You and I.* Cf. "who you shall rightly love," i. 2. 32, and "not I" for "not me," in 21 above. See also *Oth.* iv. 2. 3: "you have seen Cassio and she together." This disregard of the inflections of pronouns was common in writers of the time.

Scene III. — 9. *Naughty.* This word was formerly used in a much stronger sense than at present. In *Much Ado*, v. 1. 306 the villain Borachio is called a "naughty man"; and Gloster, in *Lear*, iii. 7. 37, when the cruel Regan plucks his beard, addresses her as "Naughty lady ! " Cf. *Proverbs*, vi. 12, etc. See also v. 1. 91 below.

Fond. Foolish; as in ii. 9. 26 above. This was the original sense of the word, and is often found in S.

10. *To come.* That is, *as* to come. Cf. *Rich. III.* iii. 2. 26 : —

> " I wonder he is so fond
> To trust the mockery of unquiet slumbers."

14. *Dull-eyed.* Wanting in perception, stupid; not with eyes dimmed with tears, as some make it.

19. *Kept.* Kept company, dwelt. Cf. *L. L. L.* iv. 1. 100, etc.

23. *Made moan.* See on i. 1. 126 above.

25. *Grant this forfeiture to hold.* Allow it to hold good.

26. *Deny the course of law.* Interfere with it, refuse to let it take its course. See on iii. 2. 284 above.

27. *For the commodity*, etc. For if the advantages heretofore enjoyed by strangers in Venice be refused them, it will seriously impeach the justice of the state. See on i. 1. 178 above.

32. *Bated.* Reduced, lowered. Cf. "bated breath," i. 3. 120 above. It should not be printed *'bated*, since it is not a mere metrical contraction of *abated*, but a distinct word (cf. *wake* and *awake*, etc.) often found in prose writers.

35. *Pray God.* The subject is omitted, as even now in "Would to God," etc.

SCENE IV. — 2. *Conceit.* Conception, notion.

6. *Send relief.* For the omission of the preposition, see on i. 1. 125 above.

7. *Lover.* Friend. So just below, "bosom lover." Cf. *J. C.* iii. 2. 13: "Romans, countrymen, and lovers." See also *Psalms*, xxxviii. 11. The word, moreover, was formerly applied to both sexes, as *paramour* and *villain* were. Even now we say of a man and woman that they are lovers, or a pair of lovers.

9. *Than customary bounty*, etc. Than ordinary benevolence can constrain you to be.

11. *Nor shall not.* See on i. 2. 26 above. *Companion* was sometimes used contemptuously, as *fellow* still is. See *J. C.* iv. 3. 138: "Companion, hence!" etc.

12. *Waste.* Spend. Cf. Milton (*Sonnet to Mr. Lawrence*): "Help waste a sullen day"; where, however, the idea of "killing time" is more evident than here.

14. *Be needs.* Just below we have the more familiar *needs be*. For *needs*, see on ii. 4. 29 above.

25. *Husbandry.* Stewardship. Cf. *T. of A.* ii. 2. 164: "If you suspect my husbandry," etc.

Manage. Cf. *Temp.* i. 2. 70: "The manage of my state." The word is especially used of horses; as in 1 *Hen. IV.* ii. 3. 52: "Speak terms of manage to thy bounding steed," etc.

28. *Contemplation.* Metrically five syllables.

30. *Her husband,* etc. An ellipsis like those in ii. 1. 46 and iii. 2. 288 above. Cf. *Hen. VIII.* ii. 3. 16: "As soul and body's severing," etc.

33. *Deny this imposition.* Refuse this charge *laid upon* you. See on i. 2. 105 above.

45. *Balthasar.* This name (sometimes *Balthazar*) is found also in *C. of E., R. and J.,* and *Much Ado,* and is always accented on the first syllable.

46. *As I have ever found thee,* etc. *Thou* and *thee* are generally used in addressing servants, and in affectionate familiarity with relatives and friends. Portia generally addresses Nerissa, who is a waiting-gentlewoman, not an ordinary servant, with *you,* but sometimes, as in i. 2 and here (62, 79), with *thou.* When *you* is used with a servant it generally implies anger or reproof.

50. *Cousin's hand.* The word *cousin* in that day was often used instead of our *kinsman* and *kinswoman.*

52. *With imagin'd speed.* With the speed of thought. Cf. *Hen. V.* iii. chor. 1: "Thus with imagin'd wing our swift scene flies."

53. *Tranect.* The word occurs nowhere else. It may be a misprint for "traject," the English equivalent of the French *trajet,* Italian *traghetto.* Coryat (*Crudities,* 1611) says: "There are in Venice thirteen ferries or passages, which they commonly call *Traghetti,* where passengers may be transported in a gondola to what place of the city they will."

56. *Convenient.* Proper, suitable. See on ii. 8. 45 above.

59. *Of us.* That is, of our seeing them.

61. *Accomplished.* Furnished. Cf. *Rich. II.* ii. 1. 177: " Ac-

complish'd with the number of thy hours"; that is, when he was of thy age. See also *Hen. V.* iv. chor. 12: "The armourers accomplishing (that is, equipping) the knights."

65. *Braver.* Finer, more showy. Both *brave* and *bravery* are often used in this sense with reference to dress, personal appearance, etc. See *Temp.* i. 2. 6, 411, ii. 2. 122, iii. 2. 12, etc. Cf. *Isaiah,* iii. 18. The Scottish *braw* is the same word.

67. *Mincing.* This word was not always contemptuous. In the one instance in which Milton uses it (*Comus,* 964: "the mincing Dryades") it appears to mean tripping lightly or gracefully. Cf. also Drayton, *Polyolb.* Song 27: "Ye maids, the hornpipe then so mincingly that tread."

69. *Quaint.* Ingenious, elaborate. See on ii. 4. 6 above.

72. *I could not do withal.* I could not help it. In Palgrave's *Lesclaircissement de la Lang. Fr.,* 1530, we find it thus explained: "*I can nat do withall,* a thyng lyeth nat in me, or I am nat in faulte that a thyng is done."

75. *That men.* This omission of *so* before *that* is very common. See *J. C.* i. 1. 50: "That Tiber trembled"; *Macb.* ii. 2. 7: "That death and nature do contend," etc.

77. *Raw.* Crude, or, in Yankee parlance, "green." Cf. *A. Y. L.* iii. 2. 76: "Thou art raw," etc.

Jacks. A common term of contempt. See *Much Ado,* v. 1. 91, *Rich. III.* i. 3. 72, etc.

79. *All my whole.* Cf. 1 *Hen. VI.* i. 1. 126: "All the whole army"; *Hen. VIII.* i. 1. 12: "All the whole time," etc.

SCENE V. — 3. *I fear you.* That is, fear *for* you; as in iii. 2. 29 above and in 29 below. Cf. *Rich. III.* i. 1. 137: "his physicians fear him mightily."

4. *Agitation.* The clown's blunder for *cogitation.*

14. *When I shun Scylla,* etc. In the *Alexandreis* of Philip Gaultier, written in the early part of the thirteenth century, we find the line, "Incidis in Scyllam, cupiens vitare Charybdim," which had

been often quoted and translated by English writers before the time of S.

20. *Enow.* A form of *enough*, generally plural. Cf. iv. 1. 29 below.

43. *Cover.* Launcelot quibbles on the two meanings of the word, *to lay the table* and *to wear one's hat* (see above, ii. 9. 43: "How many then should cover," etc.).

47. *Quarrelling with occasion.* Quibbling on every opportunity.

57. *Discretion.* Discrimination. *Suited* = suited to each other, arranged.

60. *A many.* This expression is obsolete, though we still say *a few*, and *many a* in a distributive sense. It is occasionally used in poetry, as by Gerald Massey (*Love's Fairy Ring*) : —

> "We've known a many sorrows, Sweet:
>   We've wept a many tears."

See also Tennyson (*Miller's Daughter*) : "They have not shed a many tears."

61. *Garnish'd.* Furnished, equipped.

For a tricksy word, etc. For a quibbling word (or a play upon words), set the meaning at defiance.

62. *How cheer'st thou?* Equivalent to "What cheer ? How is 't with you?" in *W. T.* i. 2. 148.

63. *Good sweet.* No term of compliment or endearment did more service in that day than *sweet*. This combination of *good sweet* occurs in *Cor.* i. 3, 119, *M. W.* iv. 2. 189, etc. *Opinion* is here a quadrisyllable, as in i. 1. 102.

69. *Mean it.* That is, intend to *live an upright life*.

74. *Pawn'd.* Staked, wagered. Cf. *Cor.* iii. 1. 15, *Cymb.* i. 4. 118, etc.

81. *Howsoe'er.* The folio has "how som ere"—a common vulgarism in that day.

ACT IV

SCENE I. — 5. *Uncapable*. S. uses both *incapable* (six times) and *uncapable* (twice). So we find *uncertain* and *incertain*, *unconstant* and *inconstant*, *unfortunate* and *infortunate*, *ungrateful* and *ingrateful*, etc.

6. *From*. S. generally has *empty of*. This is the only instance of *empty from*.

7. *Qualify*. Moderate, temper; as often.

8. *Obdurate*. The accent is on the penult, as always in S.

9. *And that*. Here *that* is omitted after *since*, and is then inserted in the second clause without *since*. This is a common construction in the Elizabethan writers. In most cases the subjects of the clauses are different. Cf. *T. and C.* ii. 2. 177: —

> " *If* this law
> Of nature be corrupted through affection,
> And *that* great minds," etc.

On the use of *that* with *if, since, when*, etc., see on ii. 6. 54 above.

10. *Envy's*. See on iii. 2. 277 above. Cf. *Mark*, xv. 10.

18. *Lead'st this fashion*, etc. You keep up this show of malice only until the final hour of execution.

20. *Remorse*. Relenting, pity. This is its usual meaning in S. Cf. *K. John*, ii. 1. 478: "Soft petitions, pity, and remorse," etc. So *remorseful* = compassionate, and *remorseless* = pitiless (as at present).

22. *Where*. Whereas. Cf. *T. G. of V.* iii. 1. 74: "Where I thought the remnant of mine age," etc.; *L. L. L.* ii. 1. 103: "Where now his knowledge must prove ignorance"; *Cor.* i. 10. 13: "Where I thought to crush him," etc. On the other hand, *whereas* sometimes = *where*, as in *2 Hen. VI.* i. 2. 58: "Whereas the king and queen do mean to hawk."

24. *Loose*. Release, remit.

26. *Moiety.* Portion, share (not an exact half); as often in S. Cf. *Ham.* i. I. 90: "a moiety competent" (a proper share), etc.

29. *Royal merchant.* This epithet was striking and well understood in S.'s time, when Sir Thomas Gresham was honoured with the title of *the royal merchant,* both from his wealth, and because he transacted the mercantile business of Queen Elizabeth; and at Venice the Giustiniani, the Grimaldi, and others were literally "merchant princes," and known as such throughout Europe. For *enow,* see on iii. 5. 20 above.

34. *Gentle.* No pun on *Gentile* is intended, as some have supposed. It could only have angered the Jew.

35. *Possess'd.* See on i. 3. 64 above.

36. *Sabbath.* One early ed. has "Sabaoth." Bacon and Spenser confound the signification of the two words, and Dr. Johnson, in the first edition of his Dictionary, treated them as identical.

39. *Your charter.* See on iii. 2. 273 above.

41. *Carrion.* A favourite term of contempt with S.

43. *But, say, it is.* But suppose it is. The commas are required to make the sense clear.

47. *Some men there are love not.* The relative is omitted, as often. *A gaping pig* is either a pig brought to table with a lemon or apple in its mouth, or the living, squealing animal.

49. *Masters of passion.* Agencies (such as he has been speaking of) that move either the sympathy or antipathy of any man. *Passion* is used in the original sense of *feeling* or *emotion.* Cf. *J. C.* i. 2. 48: "I have much mistook your passion," etc.

52. *Abide.* Bear, endure. Cf. *Temp.* i. 2. 360: "which good natures Could not abide to be with," etc.

55. *Lodg'd.* Settled, abiding.

59. *Current.* Persistent course.

65. *Think you question.* Consider that you are arguing with.

67. *Main flood.* The "ocean tide." Cf. "the flood," i. I. 10. "The main" generally means the sea (as in *Rich. III.* i. 4. 20: "tumbling billows of the main"), but sometimes the main land.

Cf. *Ham*. iv. 4. 15: "the main of Poland," and *Lear*, iii. 1. 6: "swell the curled waters 'bove the main."

77. *With all brief and plain conveniency.* With all proper brevity and directness.

78. *Have judgment.* Receive sentence. Cf. *Luke*, xix. 22.

87. *Parts.* Capacities, employments.

99. *Upon my power.* By virtue of my prerogative.

101. *Determine.* Decide. The word sometimes means *to put an end to*, as in 2 *Hen. IV*. iv. 5. 82: "Till his friend sickness hath determin'd me"; sometimes, *to come to an end*, as in *Cor*. v. 3. 120: "till these wars determine."

118. *Not on thy sole, but on thy soul.* Cf. the quibble in *J. C.* i. 1. 15: "a mender of bad soles." For the sentiment, cf. 2. *Hen. IV*. iv. 5. 107: —

> "Thou hid'st a thousand daggers in thy thoughts,
> Which thou hast whetted on thy stony heart."

120. *The hangman's axe.* So in Fletcher's *Prophetess*, iii. 2, Dioclesian, who had *stabbed* Aper, is called "the hangman of Volusius Aper"; and in *Jacke Drums Entertainment* (1616), when Brabant Junior says, "let mine owne hand Be mine owne hangman," he refers to *stabbing* himself. In the Duke of Buckingham's *Rehearsal*, Bayes speaks of "a great huge hangman, . . . with his sword drawn." In *Much Ado* (iii. 2. 11) Cupid is called "the little hangman."

121. *Envy.* Malice. See on iii. 2. 277 above.

124. *For thy life.* For allowing thee to live.

126. *Pythagoras.* The philosopher of Samos, to whom was attributed the doctrine of the transmigration of souls. Cf. *T. N.* iv. 2. 54: "*Clown.* What is the opinion of Pythagoras concerning wild-fowl? *Malvolio.* That the soul of our grandam might haply inhabit a bird."

129. *Hang'd for human slaughter.* According to Jewish law (*Exodus*, xxi. 28), an ox that gored a man to death was stoned.

In the Middle Ages animals that had injured or killed human beings were often tried and executed. Many instances of such judicial proceedings in the fourteenth and fifteenth centuries are mentioned by Baring-Gould in his *Curiosities of Olden Times* (1896). In 1386 a judge at Falaise condemned a sow to be hanged for having lacerated and killed a child. In 1389 a horse was tried and condemned to die for killing a man. In 1499 a bull was similarly sentenced at Couroy, near Beauvais, for causing the death of a boy. The trials, which were conducted with all the formalities, were sometimes before the ordinary courts, sometimes before the ecclesiastical ones. In some cases, appeals to a higher court were made, and decided in due form. During the witch persecutions in Salem, Mass., dogs were hanged for supposed complicity with persons accused.

133. *Starv'd.* The word originally meant to die, but in the latter part of the sixteenth century came to be used in the narrower sense of perishing with *cold* — a meaning which it still has in the North of England (see 2 *Hen. VI.* iii. 1. 343, etc.) — or with *hunger*.

143. *Go give.* Cf. "come view," ii. 7. 43; "go sleep," *Rich. II.* iv. 1. 139; "go seek the king," *Ham.* ii. 1. 101, etc.

154. *To fill up.* To fulfil.

156. *No impediment to let him lack.* No hindrance to his receiving. Of this peculiar form of "double negative" (which it virtually is) there are several instances in S.

164. *The difference*, etc. The dispute which is the subject of the present trial.

166. *Throughly.* See on ii. 7. 42 above.

171. *Such rule.* Such due form.

173. *Within his danger.* Cf. *V. and A.* 639: "Come not within his danger," etc.

177. *The quality of mercy*, etc. The very nature of mercy excludes the idea of compulsion.

178. *It droppeth*, etc. Cf. *Ecclesiasticus*, xxxv. 20: "Mercy is seasonable in the time of affliction, as clouds of rain in the time of drought."

183. *Shows.* Represents. Cf. *Rich. II.* iii. 4. 42 : " Showing, as in a model, our firm estate."

189. *Show.* Show itself, appear. Cf. ii. 2. 186 above.

190. *Seasons.* Tempers. Cf. *Edward III.* (1596):

> " And kings approach the nearest unto God
> By giving life and safety unto men."

193. *We do pray for mercy,* etc. S. probably had the Lord's Prayer immediately in his mind, but the sentiment is also found in *Ecclesiasticus,* xxviii.

197. *Follow.* Insist upon.

201. *Discharge.* Pay. See on iii. 2. 268 above.

203. *Twice.* Some critics would change this to *thrice,* because we have " thrice the sum " just below, but there is no necessity for bringing the two passages into mathematical agreement. S. is often careless in these little arithmetical matters.

207. *Truth.* Honesty. So " a true man " was an honest man, as opposed to a thief. See *M. for M.* iv. 2. 46 : " Every true man's apparel fits your thief "; 1 *Hen. IV.* ii. 2. 98 : " the thieves have bound the true men," etc.

216. *A Daniel come to judgment.* The allusion is to the *History of Susanna,* 45 : " The Lord raised up the holy spirit of a young youth, whose name was Daniel," etc. See also *Ezekiel,* xxviii. 3, and *Daniel,* vi. 3.

241. *Hath full relation,* etc. Clearly recognizes that this penalty (like any other) should be paid.

244. *More elder.* Double comparatives and superlatives are common in the Elizabethan writers. In S. we find " more larger " (*A. and C.* iii. 6. 76), " more better " (*Temp.* i. 2. 19), " most boldest " (*J. C.* iii. 1. 121), " most unkindest " (*Id.* iii. 2. 187), etc. In *Rich. II.* ii. 1. 49 we find " less happier," the only instance with *less* found in S.

248. *Balance.* A contracted plural, as the verb and *them* in Shylock's answer prove. Such plurals often occur (as also do pos-

sessive cases) with nouns ending in a sibilant sound; as *horse, sense, place, service,* etc.

250. *On your charge.* At your expense.

261. *Still her use.* Ever her custom. See on i. 1. 17 above. On *use,* cf. *J. C.* ii. 2. 25: "these things are beyond all use."

265. *Such misery. Misery* may have the accent on the penult both here and in *K. John,* iii. 4: "And buss thee as thy wife. Misery's love," etc.

268. *Speak me fair in death.* Speak well of me when I am dead. "Romeo that spoke him fair" (*R. and J.* iii. 1. 158) means "Romeo that spoke *to* him in conciliatory terms;" and this is the usual meaning of the phrase.

270. *A love.* Cf. *lover* in iii. 4. 17 above.

274. *With all my heart.* Cf. *Rich. II.* ii. 1. 74 fol., where the dying Gaunt jests on his name; and where, in reply to Richard's question, "Can sick men play so nicely with their names?" he says: "No, *misery makes sport to mock itself.*" The pun is the only one that Antonio utters. He treats the matter lightly in the hope of making his friend feel it less.

276. *Which is as dear.* See on ii. 7. 4 above.

288. *These be.* See on i. 3. 22 above.

289. *Barrabas.* So spelled and accented (on first syllable) in the time of S. In Marlowe's *Jew of Malta* the name is *Barabas,* not *Barabbas.*

291. *Pursue.* Accented on the first syllable. Cf. *pursuit* in *Sonn.* 143. 4.

304. *Confiscate.* Confiscated. This Latinism is most frequent in verbs derived from the first conjugation (as *dedicate, consecrate, degenerate, suffocate,* etc.), but it is found in other Latin derivatives.

321. *The substance.* The amount.

327. *I have thee on the hip.* See on i. 3. 46 above.

340. *The law hath yet another hold on you.* S. is not willing to let the case depend on the legal quibbles which he takes from the old stories (their omission would have been resented by the theatre-

goers of that day), but adds the sound law of this speech, which is entirely his own.

342. *Alien.* A trisyllable. See on i. 1. 8 above.

345. *Contrive.* Plot. Cf. *J. C.* ii. 3. 16: "the fates with traitors do contrive," etc.

365. *Which humbleness,* etc. Which humble entreaty on thy part may induce me to commute for a fine.

366. *Ay, for the state,* etc. That is, the half which goes to the state may be thus commuted, but not Antonio's.

376. *In use.* In trust for Shylock, for the purpose of securing it at his death to Lorenzo. *Use* does not mean *interest,* which Antonio has said (i. 3. 61 above) that he neither gives nor takes.

382. *Of all he dies possess'd.* See on i. 1. 125 above.

392. *Ten more.* To make up a jury of twelve. This appears to have been an old joke. Of course it is out of place here, as trial by jury was unknown in Venice.

395. *Desire your grace of pardon.* Cf. *M. N. D.* iii. 1. 185: "desire you of more acquaintance;" and *Oth.* iii. 3. 212: "beseech you of your pardon."

399. *Gratify.* Recompense. Cf. *Cor.* ii. 2. 44: "To gratify his noble service," etc.

405. *Cope.* Reward, requite.

414. *Of force.* Of necessity. *Perforce* is still used in this sense.
Attempt. Tempt. Cf. *M. for M.* iv. 2. 205: "neither my coat, integrity, nor persuasion can with ease attempt you."

444. *Commandement.* The spelling in all the early eds. The word is also a quadrisyllable in 1 *Hen. VI.* i. 3. 20: "From him I have express commandement."

Scene II. — 6. *Upon more advice.* Upon further consideration. Cf. *M. for M.* v. 1. 469: "after more advice"; and *Rich. II.* i. 3. 233: "upon good advice" (after due deliberation), etc.

15. *Old swearing.* *Old* in this intensive or augmentative sense is common in writers of the time. For other examples in S., see

Macb. ii. 3. 2, *M. W.* i. 4. 5, *Much Ado*, v. 2. 98, and 2 *Hen. IV.* ii.
4. 21.   Cf. the slang phrase of our day, " a high old time," and other
familiar uses of *old* (" old fellow," " old boy," etc.).

ACT V

SCENE I. — 4. *Troilus.*   S. in the play of *Troilus and Cressida*
makes " Cressid " the daughter of the soothsayer Calchas, but her
name is not found in classic fable.   The allusion here is borrowed
from Chaucer's *Troilus and Cresseide*, in which the prince is
described as watching " upon the walles " for Cressida's coming.

7. *Thisbe.*   The story of the Babylonian lovers, Pyramus and
Thisbe, is told by Ovid.   Golding's translation was published in
1564, but S. may have read the original.   He probably drew more
directly from Chaucer's *Legende of Goode Women*, in which Thisbe,
Dido, and Medea are introduced one after another.   He had already
used the story in the *M. N. D.*

10. *Dido.*   The picture of Dido is not in accordance with Virgil's
narrative.   It may have been suggested by that of Ariadne in the
Legende of Goode Women (2187 fol.) : —

> " to the stronde barefote fast she went. —
> *   *   *   *   *
> Hire kerchefe on a pole styked shee,
> Ascaunce that he shulde hyt wel ysee,
> And hym remembre that she was behynde,
> And turn agayne, and on the stronde hire fynde."

The earliest reference to the *willow* as a symbol of forsaken love
is found in a manuscript collection of poems by John Heywood,
about 1530.   Cf. *Much Ado*, ii. 1. 194, 225, *Oth.* iv. 3. 28 fol.,
3 *Hen. VI.* iii. 3. 228, etc.

11. *Waft.*   For *wafted*, as in *K. John*, ii. 1. 73: "Than now the
English bottoms have waft o'er."   Cf. *lift* for *lifted* in 1 *Hen. VI.*
i. 1. 16, *Genesis*, vii. 17, *Psalms*, xciii. 3, etc.

13. *Medea.* The allusion is to the fable of her restoring Æson, the father of Jason, to youthful vigour by her enchantments. Ovid tells us that she drew blood from his veins, and supplied its place with the juice of certain herbs.

16. *Unthrift.* We have the adjective again in *T. of A.* iv. 3. 311, and the noun in *Rich. II.* ii. 3. 122, *Sonn.* 9. 9 and 13. 13.

28. *Stephano.* In the *Temp.* (written ten or more years later) this name has the accent on the first syllable, where it belongs.

31. *Holy crosses.* These are very common in Italy. There is a shrine of the Madonna del Mare in the midst of the sea between Mestre and Venice, and another between Venice and Palestrina, where the gondolier and mariner cross themselves in passing.

36. *Go we in.* See on ii. 8. 53 above. In "let us prepare," in the next line, we have the ordinary form of the 1st pers. imperative.

39. *Sola,* etc. An imitation of the post-horn.

41. *Master Lorenzo,* etc. The early eds. have " M. Lorenzo, M. Lorenzo," " M. Lorenzo & M. Lorenzo," and " M. Lorenzo and Mrs. Lorenza."

53. *Music.* This word sometimes meant musical instruments, or a band of music. See *Hen. VIII.* iv. 2. 94: " Bid the music leave ; They are harsh," etc. Cf. 98 below: " It is your music, madam, of the house."

56. *Creep in. In* was often used for *into.*

59. *Patines.* The *patine* was the plate used for the sacramental bread, and was sometimes made of gold. Some editors prefer " patterns," the reading of the 2d folio.

61. *His motion. His* for *its,* as in 82 below. See on iii. 2. 82 above. For other allusions to the " music of the spheres " in S., see *A. and C.* v. 2. 84, *T. N.* iii. 1. 121, *A. Y. L.* ii. 7. 6, etc.

62. *Cherubins.* The singular *cherubin* is found in *Temp.* i. 2. 152, *Macb.* i. 7. 22, *Oth.* iv. 2. 62, and *L. C.* 319 ; *cherub* only in *Ham.* iv. 3. 50. *Cherubin* occurs in Spenser and other poets of the time, and is used even by Dryden.

63. *Such harmony,* etc. Besides the music of the spheres, which

no mortal ear ever caught a note of, there was by some philosophers supposed to be a harmony in the human soul. "Touching musical harmony," says Hooker, "whether by instrument or by voice, it being but of high and low sounds in a due proportionable disposition, such, notwithstanding, is the force thereof, and so pleasing effects it hath in that very part of man which is most divine, that some have been thereby induced to think that the soul itself, by nature is, or hath in it, harmony." But, though this harmony is within us, "this muddy vesture of decay," as the poet tells us, "doth grossly close it in" so that we cannot hear it.

72. *Unhandled colts.* Cf. Ariel's simile of the "unback'd colts," *Temp.* iv. 1. 176.

77. *Mutual.* Common. Cf. *M. N. D.* iv. 1. 122: "mutual cry," etc. The confounding of *mutual* and *common* (as in "mutual friend," etc.) is a familiar blunder nowadays.

79. *The poet.* Probably Ovid, who tells the story in his *Metamorphoses.*

80. *Orpheus.* Cf. *T. G. of V.* iii. 2. 78: —

> "For Orpheus' lute was strung with poet's sinews,
>   Whose golden touch could soften steel and stones," etc.;

and *Hen. VIII.* iii. 1. 3: —

> "Orpheus with his lute made trees,
>   And the mountain tops that freeze,
>   Bow themselves when he did sing."

87. *Erebus.* Cf. *J. C.* ii. 1. 84: "Not Erebus itself were dim enough," etc. The word, though sometimes used figuratively for the lower world in general, denotes strictly "a place of nether darkness between the Earth and Hades."

99. *Without respect.* Absolutely, without regard to circumstances.

103. *Attended.* Attended to, listened to attentively. Cf. *Sonn.* 102. 7: —

> " As Philomel in summer's front doth sing,
>   And stops her pipe in growth of riper days;
>   Not that the summer is less pleasant now
>   Than when her mournful hymns did hush the night,
>   But that wild music burthens every bough,
>   And sweets grown common lose their dear delight."

All the birds mentioned here — the crow, lark, cuckoo, etc. — are found in Italy.

107. *By season*, etc. " By fitness of occasion are adapted or qualified to obtain their just appreciation, and to show their true excellence."

109. *Peace, ho !* In *J. C.* i. 2. 1 we find " Peace, ho ! " used, as here, to silence the music.

Endymion. A beautiful shepherd beloved by Diana. Fletcher, in the *Faithful Shepherdess*, tells

> " How the pale Phœbe, hunting in a grove,
>   First saw the boy Endymion, from whose eyes
>   She took eternal fire that never dies;
>   How she convey'd him softly in a sleep,
>   His temples bound with poppy, to the steep
>   Head of old Latmos, where she stoops each night,
>   Gilding the mountain with her brother's light,
>   To kiss her sweetest."

The fable appears in many forms in the classic writers, and has been a favourite one with poets ever since.

115. *Which speed.* See on ii. 7. 4 above.

121. *A tucket sounds.* This stage direction is found in the 1st folio. A *tucket* (probably from the Italian *toccata*) is a flourish on a trumpet. Cf. *Hen. V.* iv. 2. 35: " Then let the trumpet sound The tucket-sonance."

127. *We should hold day*, etc. We should have day when the Antipodes do, if you, Portia, would walk abroad at night.

129. *Let me give light,* etc. See on iii. 2. 91 above. Puns on *light* and *dark* and *light* and *heavy* are frequent in S.

132. *God sort all!* God dispose all things! Cf. *Rich. III.* ii. 3. 36:—

> "All may be well; but if God sort it so,
> 'T is more than we deserve or I expect."

136. *In all sense.* In all reason.

141. *Breathing courtesy.* Cf. *Macb.* v. 3. 27: "Mouth-honour, breath."

146. *Poesy.* The *poesy* or *posy* (for the two words are the same) of a ring was a motto or rhyme inscribed upon its inner side. The fashion of putting such "posies" on rings prevailed from the middle of the sixteenth to the close of the seventeenth centuries. In 1624 a little book was published with the quaint title, *Love's Garland, or Posies for Rings, Handkerchiefs, and Gloves; and such pretty tokens, that lovers send their loves.* Cf. *Ham.* iii. 2. 162: "Is this a prologue, or the poesy of a ring?" These are the only instances in which S. uses the word in this sense.

148. *Leave me not.* Do not part with me. *Leave* is used in the same sense by Portia in 170 below.

154. *Respective.* Considerate, regardful. Cf. *R. and J.* iii. 1. 128: "respective lenity." See also *K. John,* i. 1. 188.

156. *On 's.* See on ii. 6. 67 above.

160. *Scrubbed.* Stunted, dwarfish; generally used contemptuously.

175. *I were best.* See on ii. 8. 33 above.

191. *The ring.* For the repetition in this and the following speech, Herford compares *K. John,* iii. 1. 12–15 and *Rich. III.* i. 3. 292–294. See also *Edward III.* ii. 1. 155–163, where nine lines end with "the sun."

197. *The virtue of the ring.* The power it has; the right to me and mine of which it is the pledge. See iii. 2. 171, where Portia gives the ring.

199. *Contain.* Retain; as in *Sonn.* 77. 9: "what thy memory

cannot contain," etc. *Your honour* refers to his pledge in iii. 2. 183.

202. *Had pleas'd to have defended.* For "had pleased to defend." The inaccuracy is sometimes found in good writers of our day, and has sometimes been defended by grammarians.

203. *Wanted.* As to have wanted.

204. *Urge.* Urge you to give it to him; insist upon it. *Ceremony* = a sacred thing.

208. *Civil doctor.* Doctor of civil law.

218. *For, by these*, etc. Cf. *R. and J.* iii. 5. 9: "Night's candles are burnt out"; *Macb.* ii. 1. 5: "There's husbandry in heaven; Their candles are all out," etc.

237. *Wealth.* Weal, prosperity; as in *Ham.* iv. 4. 27: "much wealth and peace."

238. *Which.* That is, which *loan*.

239. *Miscarried.* Perished; as in ii. 8. 29 and iii. 2. 311 above.

241. *Advisedly.* Deliberately. Cf. *advised* in i. 1. 142 and ii. 1. 42 above.

257. *Richly.* Richly laden. Cf. "richly left," i. 1. 161 above.

260. *Living.* See on *livings*, iii. 2. 156 above.

262. *To road.* To harbour. Cf. "ports, and piers, and roads," i. 1. 19 above.

270. *Satisfied of.* Satisfied concerning; that is, you wish to know more about them. *At full* = in full, fully.

272. *And charge us*, etc. "In the Court of Queen's Bench, when a complaint is made against a person for 'contempt,' the practice is that before sentence is finally pronounced he is sent into the Crown Office, and being there 'charged upon interrogatories' he is made to swear that he will 'answer all things faithfully'" (Lord Campbell's *Shakespeare's Legal Acquirements*).

Inter'gatories. This contracted form was common in S.'s time. We find it even in prose in *A. W.* iv. 3. 207, as printed in the early eds. The full form occurs in *K. John*, iii. 1. 147.

APPENDIX

COMMENTS ON SOME OF THE CHARACTERS

ANTONIO AND HIS FRIENDS. — Antonio gives the name to the play, though not in a sense its hero, because, through his relations with Bassanio and with Shylock, he is the mainspring of the action. He is one of Shakespeare's most beautiful characters. Professor Moulton (*Shakespeare as a Dramatic Artist*) calls him "a perfect character," his intolerance, interpreted in the light of his time, being a virtue rather than a fault. But it seems to me that the critic misapprehends the type of Antonio's perfection. He says that "Roman honour" is the idea which the Merchant's friends are accustomed to associate with him; and he adds: "Of all the national types of character the Roman is the most self-sufficient, alike incorruptible by temptation and independent of the softer influences of life." Antonio *is* incorruptible, the very soul of honour, and it is to this that Bassanio refers in ascribing to him the "ancient Roman honour." He would not have added the Roman sternness and impassivity, the lack of sensibility to the softer influences of life.

Mistaking Antonio in this way, Professor Moulton naturally does injustice to the group of friends with whom we find him associated in the opening scene. Here, he says, "we see the dignified merchant-prince suffering under the infliction of frivolous visitors, to which his friendship with the young nobleman exposes him." The German Gervinus in like manner regards these friends, Bassanio included, as mere parasites; and Heine terms them "only so-called friends, or, if you please, only half or three-quarters friends," having "due regard to their own ease," in their apparent devotion to "the excellent merchant who gave them such fine dinners."

There may be nothing in the first scene which makes it abso-lutely certain that Antonio's friends are not selfish "summer friends" (such as the dramatist introduces in *Timon of Athens*); but elsewhere in the play the question is settled past a doubt. Their love for him endures the crucial test of adversity. When news of the loss of his ships begins to come (ii. 8) Salanio says to Salarino: —

> "You were best to tell Antonio what you hear;
> Yet do not suddenly, for it may grieve him;"

and his friend replies: "A kinder gentleman treads not the earth." Then follows that exquisite passage in which the parting of Antonio and Bassanio is described; and Salanio adds: —

> "I think he only loves the world for him.
> I pray thee, let us go and find him out,
> And quicken his embraced heaviness
> With some delight or other."

Later on (iii. 1), when more bad news comes and Antonio is threatened with bankruptcy, the devotion of these friends is none the less to be noted — and, as in the former instance, when they are by themselves, and can have no motive for playing a false part. Salanio speaks of the Merchant as "the good Antonio — O that I had a title good enough to keep his name company!" Gratiano also calls him "the good Antonio," and in the trial scene he cannot find language intense enough to express his grief and wrath on account of the Jew's merciless spite against Antonio, and his exult-ant irony when the Daniel come to judgment has decided in favour of the Merchant. Can these be parasitical friends?

Antonio has been often called a "melancholy" man, but he is not such by nature, though grave and earnest. At the opening of the play the shadow of coming misfortune already hangs over him. He is sad, he knows not why, but it is the poet's fondness for pre-sentiments that has made him so. It surprises his friends, which, no less than his own comments upon it, indicates that it is not his ordinary mood. We are sure that he must be usually genial, or he could not attract these lively young men, who, as we have seen, are no parasites; and we infer from their talk that he can even be merry at times, though probably in no boisterous way.

In but one instance (see note on iv. 1. 274) does he indulge in a pun, and it is the most pathetic pun in all Shakespeare. It is in what he supposes is to be his last speech before he dies: —

> " Repent not you that you shall lose your friend,
>   And he repents not that he pays your debt;
>   For if the Jew do cut but deep enough,
>   I 'll pay it instantly *with all my heart*."

He puns that never punned before, out of pure love and pity for his friend, whom he would fain keep from grieving at his death. And this is the man who has been called " insensible to the softer influences of life ! "

In the last scene of the play, where we see Antonio relieved from the anxiety of the past two or three months, he has little to say, but that little is in the same unselfish vein. He is troubled at the apparent misunderstanding about the rings, and says, " I am the unhappy subject of these quarrels "; and he tries to make peace by offering to become surety for Bassanio's good faith in the future.

This man, as I have said, is a favourite with Shakespeare, but Shakespeare is never afraid to show the faults and weaknesses of his best characters. *He* did not regard Antonio's treatment of the Jew as a " virtue," although that was the medieval view of it. Here, as everywhere, he holds the mirror up to nature, letting it reflect the age as it was. If we consider what was then the general feeling towards the Jews, and with what bitter contempt and detestation they were regarded, even by the best Christians, how they were abused, robbed, and persecuted, we cannot wonder at the repugnance and scorn which the good Antonio manifests towards Shylock — that he calls him " dog," and spits upon him. When the Jew reminds him of these " courtesies " at the time when he is asking the loan, Antonio replies: —

> "I am as like to call thee so again,
> To spet on thee again, to spurn thee too.
> If thou wilt lend this money, lend it not
> As to thy friends; for when did friendship take
> A breed of barren metal of his friend?
> But lend it rather to thine enemy,
> Who if he break, thou mayst with better face
> Exact the penalty."

Shakespeare meant that Antonio should remember that speech — and that we should remember it — when later he is fain to beg mercy of the "dog" he has despised and defied, and gets for answer: —

> "Thou call'dst me dog before thou hadst a cause;
> But, since I am a dog, beware my fangs."

SHYLOCK. — There are those who believe that Shakespeare shared the prejudice of his time against the Jew; but to me nothing can be clearer than that he has indirectly — and the more effectively because indirectly — exposed and reproved its injustice. Here, as so often in his works, he proves himself far in advance of his age. Shylock is thwarted and punished, as he deserved to be; but he shows his Christian adversaries that they have taught him the lesson of revenge; that if the Jewish maxim be "an eye for an eye, and a tooth for a tooth," it has been fully indorsed and adopted by the Christian — an iron rule in place of his professed golden one. "If you wrong us," he reasons, "shall we not revenge? If we are like you in the rest, we will resemble you in that. If a Jew wrong a Christian, what is his humility? Revenge. If a Christian wrong a Jew, what should his sufferance be, by Christian example? Why, revenge. The villany you teach me, I will execute; and it shall go hard but I will better the instruction."

There is no possible answer to this, and it is a most significant fact that Shakespeare makes his Christians attempt none. Shylock is left master of the field; and this is the method the poet chooses for reading a high moral lesson to the men of his time. Had he ventured to do it more openly and directly, the play would have been hooted from the stage.

It is safe, I think, to say that a decided majority of the commentators and critics are now agreed that Shakespeare's sympathies are with Shylock as the representative of a wronged and persecuted race; and some of those on the other side appear to be there solely because, as they say, Shakespeare was a dramatist and not a moral teacher; or, as one of them expresses it, " he was too thoroughly an artist to write a play with a moral purpose." Another says that, if he had intended to enforce the lesson of toleration and charity with regard to the Jews, he would not have selected " a rich merchant plotting the murder of a Christian rival by means of a fraudulent contract "; nor would he have made Shylock argue that " Jews had a right to turn devils as freely as Christians had."

The answer to all this is easy and simple. Shakespeare did *not* write the play to enforce the moral lesson. His purpose was to dramatize a story, or combination of stories, which he found ready to his hand, or which may have been suggested to him by the manager of a theatre. But in depicting the Jew in the story he saw him and his race as they were, not as they appeared to the Christians of his time. He saw all that was bad in Shylock, but he saw as well that the evil in him was mainly due to the treatment he had received at the hands of the Christians. He *was* too great a master of his art to preach his moral; and he knew that there was no necessity for doing it. He simply sets the Jew himself before us as he is, nothing extenuating but setting down naught in malice, and the man gains our sympathy at once and inevitably. Heine says: " When I saw this play at Drury Lane, there stood behind me in the box a pale, fair Briton who, at the end of the fourth act, fell to weeping passionately, exclaiming several times, ' The poor man is wronged!' It was a face of the noblest Grecian type, and the eyes were large and black. I have never been able to forget those large and black eyes that wept for Shylock." We may not weep with the fair English girl, but we cannot help sharing her pity and sympathy for Shylock; and in this result the genius of the poet, or, as Heine expresses it, " the genius of humanity that reigned in him," is triumphant over vulgar prejudice and fanaticism.

It would take too much space to explain in detail how Shakespeare accomplishes this in his delineation of the Jew: by making him one of his most intellectual characters; by giving him a generous enthusiasm for his ancient race, religion, and law; and by little touches showing that he is not destitute of tenderness, or at least of reminiscences of tenderness, as when he mourns the loss of the ring that Leah gave him when he was a bachelor. There was one soft spot in his heart, though the rest might be as hard as Gratiano intimated when he exclaimed, while Shylock was whetting his knife in the trial scene: —

> " Not on thy sole, but on thy soul, harsh Jew,
> Thou mak'st thy knife keen."

If the reader would understand better that Shylock is what he is because Shakespeare was what we know him to be, — a poet not for an age, but for all time, — let him read Marlowe's *Jew of Malta*, and compare the hero with Shylock. The latter, with all his avarice and cruelty, is a *man ;* the former is an impossible *monster*, who boasts that he " walks abroad o' nights, and kills sick persons groaning under walls "; poisons wells, and studies physic that he may keep the sextons busy " with digging graves and ringing dead men's knells "; by his extortions fills jails with bankrupts, and hospitals with orphans; chuckles when his victims hang themselves in their despair; and finally dies unrepentant and defiant, with curses on his lips against these enemies and infidels. But this is the ideal Jew of Marlowe's and Shakespeare's generation !

And Martin Luther was no less prejudiced and intolerant. He wrote thus: " Know, thou dear Christian, that, next to the devil, thou canst have no bitterer, fiercer foe than a genuine Jew, one who is a Jew in earnest. The true counsel I give thee is that fire be put to their synagogues, and that, over what will not burn up, the earth be heaped and piled, so that no stone or trace of them be seen forevermore." [1]

PORTIA. — About Portia there has been, and can be, but little room for critics to differ and dispute. They are few who do not cordially agree with Mrs. Kemble that she is "the ideal of the perfect woman" — that she realizes Wordsworth's description of such —

> "A perfect woman, nobly planned
> To warn, to comfort, and command,"

and yet —

> "A creature not too bright or good
> For human nature's daily food;
> For transient sorrows, simple wiles,
> Praise, blame, love, kisses, tears, and smiles."

She is, in the words of the same sympathetic critic, "the wise, witty woman, loving with all her soul and submitting with all her heart to a man whom everybody but herself (who was the best judge) would have judged her inferior; the laughter-loving, light-hearted, true-hearted, deep-hearted woman, full of keen perception, of active efficiency, of wisdom prompted by love, of tenderest unselfishness, of generous magnanimity; noble, simple, humble, pure; true, dutiful, religious, and full of fun; delightful above all others, the woman of women."

I quote this because, in brief compass, it brings out all the marked features of the character. What can we add to it? What can we take away? [2]

As I have hinted, a small minority of the critics have their disparaging comments on Portia. Hazlitt says that she is "not a great favourite" with him; she "has a certain degree of affectation and pedantry about her." Mr. C. A. Brown cannot go so far as

---

[1] From Furness's "New Variorum" edition of the play, p. 453.

[2] If anything, the intimation that Bassanio was not entirely worthy of Portia; but, as Mrs. Kemble admits, Portia was the best judge of that.

Hazlitt does, but thinks she is not quite so amiable as Mrs. Jameson makes her out; he calls her "a feudal lady," who seems to "rejoice in laying down the law, and feels a triumphant delight while she detains the court in suspense." Hudson considers that she is at times "too self-conscious," though he sees "nothing like ostentation or conceit of intellect" in her.

These criticisms are all in the same vein, and Hazlitt's, being the most severe, may be taken as including the rest; but Hazlitt, though an acute critic, had his moods and prejudices, and he doubtless wrote what I have quoted when he was not in the humour for appreciating a character like Portia. Certainly we can find nothing of pedantry or affectation in her, even when she is playing the doctor's part at the trial. An inferior woman, "coached" for the occasion by the learned Bellario, would have been likely to overdo the part in the endeavour to carry it out successfully and effectively. She would have behaved more like a young lawyer in all the pride of his first case in court, who felt that the aid and advice of his experienced senior had insured his success. But Portia maintains throughout the quiet dignity of a truly great lawyer, who is tempted to no affectation of learning, no display of legal acumen, but states his case clearly, simply, and briefly. The only eloquent passage in her management of the cause — using the word in its ordinary sense — is in the famous plea for mercy, which is surely not a display of rhetoric, but a natural outburst from the heart. In short, her bearing from first to last is as modest as it is dignified.

Elsewhere in the play her modest opinion of herself is repeatedly illustrated. She speaks of the suitors who come to hazard for her "worthless self"; and in that matchless speech after Bassanio has chosen the right casket, she disclaims ambition for herself, but adds: —

> "Yet for you
> I would be trebled twenty times myself,
> A thousand times more fair, ten thousand times more rich,
> That only to stand high in your account,
> I might in virtues, beauties, livings, friends,

> Exceed account. But the full sum of me
> Is sum of nothing, which, to term in gross,
> Is an unlesson'd girl, unschool'd, unpractis'd:
> Happy in this, she is not yet so old
> But she may learn ; happier than this,
> She is not bred so dull but she can learn;
> Happiest of all in that her gentle spirit
> Commits itself to yours to be directed,
> As from her lord, her governor, her king.
> Myself and what is mine to you and yours
> Is now converted. But now I was the lord
> Of this fair mansion, master of my servants,
> Queen o'er myself; and even now, but now,
> This house, these servants, and this same myself
> Are yours, my lord. I give them with this ring."

Is there any " pedantry " in that ? Is this noble heiress, who thus frankly gives herself and all that is hers to the lover who has won her, affected and vain ? The utmost that she claims for herself is that she is not so dull but she can learn — which is far enough from the pride of pedantry. Mr. Grant White was not fond of learned women, — or, at least, of a certain type of such women, — but even he does no injustice to Portia. He sums up her character in a single sentence as " the matchless impersonation of that rare woman who is gifted even more in intellect than in loveliness, and who yet stops gracefully short of the offence of intellectuality." The word *intellectuality*, as he uses it, seems to bear somewhat the same relation to *intellect* that *sentimentality* does to *sentiment*, suggesting a self-consciousness or self-conceit which is an essential element in pedantry. It carries a certain degree of reproach with it; but White is unquestionably right in acknowledging that, with all her high intellectual endowments, Portia is nowise liable to the charge of " intellectuality."

The lighter and more playful side of Portia's character is well displayed in the very first scene in which she appears. Her descriptions of the suitors are as witty as they are graphic, showing alike her insight into character and her love of fun. How completely the men are photographed in a sentence or two! The Neapolitan prince "doth nothing but talk of his horse." But a "horsey" man is not necessarily a fool, like this fellow who plumes himself on being able to shoe his horse. He is a prince, but his highest ambition is to be his own blacksmith. Do we need to know anything more about him? What a husband for the peerless Portia if the lottery of the caskets had given her to him! But, as Nerissa philosophically remarks, "holy men at their death have good inspirations," and her father's device for getting her a mate is likely to be governed by a wise Providence. She will escape this unprincely prince; and the morose and self-conceited County Palatine, like a death's head with a bone in his mouth; and the volatile French lord, who would be twenty husbands in one, and that one worthless; and the young baron of England, who has travelled in many lands and brought home nothing but his motley apparel and his mongrel behaviour; and the cowardly Scotchman, who lacks the spirit to return a blow, but swears he will do it some day; and the guzzling German, who at his best is worse than a man, and at his worst is little better than a beast. Luckily this parcel of wooers will trouble the lady with no more suit, unless she may be won otherwise than by the chance of the caskets; and we may be sure that she is sincere in wishing them a fair departure.

But, as Mrs. Jameson remarks, "all the finest parts of Portia's character are brought to bear in the trial scene"; and here I cannot do better than to go on with her admirable comments on the scene, instead of attempting to make any of my own: —

"There she shines forth, all her divine self. Her intellectual powers, her elevated sense of religion, her high honourable principles, her best feelings as a woman, are all displayed. She maintains at first a calm self-command, as one sure of carrying her point in the end; yet the painful heart-thrilling uncertainty in which she keeps the whole court until suspense verges upon agony, is not contrived for effect merely; it is necessary and inevitable. . . . Thus all the speeches addressed to Shylock in the first instance are either direct or indirect experiments on his temper and feelings. She must be understood from the beginning to the end as examining, with intense anxiety, the effect of her own words on his mind and countenance; as watching for that relenting spirit which she hopes to awaken either by reason or persuasion. She begins by an appeal to his mercy, in that matchless piece of eloquence which, with an irresistible and solemn pathos, falls upon the heart like 'gentle dew from heaven ': — but in vain; for that blessed dew drops not more fruitless and unfelt on the parched sand of the desert, than do these heavenly words upon the ear of Shylock. She next attacks his avarice : —

> "'Shylock, there's *thrice* thy money offered thee!'

Then she appeals, in the same breath, both to his avarice and his pity : —

> "'Be merciful!
> Take thrice thy money. Bid me tear the bond.'

All that she says afterwards — her strong expressions, which are calculated to strike a shuddering horror through the nerves, the reflections she interposes, her delays and circumlocution to give time for any latent feeling of commiseration to display itself, — all, all are premeditated, and tend in the same manner to the object she has in view.[1]

"So unwilling is her sanguine and generous spirit to resign all hope, or to believe that humanity is absolutely extinct in the bosom of the Jew, that she calls on Antonio, as a last resource, to speak for himself. His gentle, yet manly resignation, the deep pathos of his farewell, and the affectionate allusion to herself in his last address to Bassanio : —

> "'Commend me to your honourable wife;
> Say how I lov'd you, speak me fair in death,' etc. —

---

[1] This is a sufficient answer to Mr. C. A. Brown's criticism, that she delights in keeping the court in suspense.

are well calculated to swell that emotion which through the whole scene must have been labouring suppressed within her heart.

"At length the crisis arrives, for patience and womanhood can endure no longer; and when Shylock, carrying his savage bent 'to the last hour of act,' springs on his victim—'A sentence! come, prepare!' then the smothered scorn, indignation, and disgust burst forth with an impetuosity which interferes with the judicial solemnity she had at first affected, particularly in the speech —

"'Therefore, prepare thee to cut off the flesh,' etc.

But she afterwards recovers her propriety, and triumphs with a cooler scorn and a more self-possessed exultation.

"It is clear that, to feel the full force and dramatic beauty of this marvellous scene, we must go along with Portia as well as with Shylock ; we must understand her concealed purpose, keep in mind her noble motives, and pursue in our fancy the undercurrent of feeling working in her mind throughout. The terror and the power of Shylock's character, his deadly and inexorable malice, would be too oppressive, the pain and pity too intolerable, and the horror of the possible issue too overwhelming, but for the intellectual relief afforded by this double source of interest and contemplation."

BASSANIO. — Bassanio has been misrepresented and underrated by some of the critics, and the reason is not far to seek. In a play, as in real life, a person may have a part not at all proportionate to his abilities, and may consequently fail to be appreciated as he deserves. In the present play Portia has great and varied opportunities ; hence she can display her great and varied endowments. Bassanio, on the other hand, has nothing to do except to marry Portia, who was practically won before the play begins. The prominent part she has in the action, and the power and grace with which she discharges it, throw her husband completely into the shade. As Nerissa tells us, he is "a scholar and a soldier" (we have the ideal man of the time in that simple statement), but he has no opportunity to prove himself either soldier or scholar.

To a careless observer he seems to be, as he has often been called, a fortune-hunter ; but Shakespeare is quick to foresee any possible injustice we may do his favourite characters and to guard them well against it, and he has done so in this instance. When Bassanio tells Antonio about Portia, note how her fortune is subordinated to her beauty and her character : —

> " In Belmont is a lady richly left ;
> And she is fair and, fairer than that word,
> Of wondrous virtues."

He has met her, moreover, and, as we learn in the next scene, before her father's death ; and, like Ferdinand and Miranda in *The Tempest,* at the first sight they " changed eyes." To remove any possible doubt that the budding love was mutual, and that Bassanio had not misapprehended the " fair speechless messages " from the lady's eyes, the dramatist gives us that exquisite bit of dialogue (i. 2. 112 fol.) in which the sly Nerissa, whose feminine instinct has, perhaps, been quicker to discern the true state of the case than the lovers themselves, entraps her mistress into an involuntary betrayal of her interest in the young man : —

" *Nerissa.* Do you not remember, lady, in your father's time, a Venetian, a scholar and a soldier, that came hither in company of the Marquis of Montferrat ?

Portia. Yes, yes, it was Bassanio ; as I think, so was he called."

What significance in the duplication of that *yes !* It shows that this speech is Portia's impulsive expression of what till then had been shut up in her heart. It comes out before she is aware, and with quick maidenly shyness she withdraws again into her herself, covering the retreat by that " as I think, so was he called," — " I believe that was the man's name ! " And yet, what critic has noticed the delicate touch, or what actress ever rightly rendered it ?

We see later (iii. 2. 248 fol.) how frankly Bassanio, when he did impart his love to Portia, told her that all the wealth he had ran in his veins. Was that done like a fortune-hunter ?

But some may say that, however this may be, Bassanio is in no respect a worthy mate for Portia. They will class him with Proteus and Claudio (him of *Much Ado*) and Bertram and others, to whom Shakespeare gives wives much too good for them. For myself, I cannot put Bassanio in this ignoble company. If, as we have seen, he is the mere "walking gentleman" of the stage, he is a gentleman in the best sense of the term, a man after Shakespeare's own heart, and not unworthy of the friendship of Antonio and the love of Portia. In the matter of the caskets, as Dowden well says, "Bassanio is ennobled in our eyes by his choice; for the gold, silver, and lead, with their several inscriptions, are a test of true lovers." He "does not come as a needy adventurer to choose the golden casket, or to 'gain' or 'get' anything, but, in the true spirit of self-abandoning love, to 'give,' not to 'get,' 'and hazard all he hath'; and, having dared to give all, he gains all." And the manner in which he receives this great good gift of Fortune is characteristic. It is not the manner of the Jason who has won the golden fleece and exults in the prize. He can scarce believe that he has gained the lady, and stands bewildered, doubtful whether it can be true, until confirmed, signed, ratified by *her*. When his friends from Venice arrive a little later, what delicacy in his greeting!

> "Lorenzo and Salerio, welcome hither;
> *If that the youth of my new interest here*
> *Have power to bid you welcome. By your leave,*
> I bid my very friends and countrymen,
> Sweet Portia, welcome."

The lady had already recognized him as "her lord, her governor, her king," and had said:—

> "Myself and what is mine to you and yours
> Is now converted."

And how easily and confidently the man who had an eye to her fortune rather than to herself would have entered into possession on such a warrant! Bassanio, overwhelmed with the gift of herself, cannot yet give a thought to his rights in what is hers. Though lord of the fair mansion, the first claim upon his hospitality takes him by surprise, and he appeals to Portia for authority to exercise his newly acquired rights and privileges.

Several commentators agree in thinking that Portia selected the *Song* in this scene in order to give Bassanio a clue to the right casket. One of them remarks: " Its general purport may be stated to be : ' Do not choose by the eye — by the glittering outside — for it is the source of all delusion.' Hence Portia, after observing with the greatest care all the formalities of her father's will, breaks it just at the point of its conflict with her subjective right "; that is, her right to choose her own husband. The critic believes that she is fully justified in doing this. But she has declared in the first speech of this very scene that she will not do it : —

> " I could teach you
> How to choose right, but then I am forsworn ;
> So will I never be. So may you miss me ;
> But if you do, you'll make me wish a sin,
> That I had been forsworn."

Earlier in the play (i. 2. 106) she has said : " If I live to be as old as Sibylla, I will die as chaste as Diana, unless I be obtained by the manner of my father's will." In both cases we cannot doubt that she means what she says.

For myself I do not believe that she had anything to do with the selection of the song, which was probably left to the leader of her household band of musicians (like the music for which Lorenzo calls in v. 1. 66); but if she selected it, this was done before the scene opened, and before she declares to Bassanio that she will never " teach him how to choose right."

I suspect that it would never have occurred to the commentators that the song had a purpose if they had not been misled by the first line — the first word indeed — of Bassanio's speech that follows: "*So* may the outward shows be least themselves." But the *So* connects what he says, not with any suggestion of the song, but with what has been going on in his mind while he was studying the caskets. The thought that appearances are deceitful has already occurred to him, and he continues the train of reasoning that it starts. It is this that leads him to choose the meagre lead that rather threatens than promises aught — that bids him "give and hazard all he hath" rather than seek what many men desire, or hope to get what he may deserve. This inscription on the leaden casket is Shakespeare's own, not taken, like the others, from the old stories; and he doubtless intended that we should recognize the unselfishness of genuine love at which it hints as the clue to the right choice.

THE PRINCES OF MOROCCO AND OF ARRAGON. — The subordinate characters in the plays deserve more study than they ordinarily get. Charles Cowden-Clarke, in his *Shakespeare Characters*, takes up, as the title-page states, "chiefly those subordinate"; but the commentators generally have not much to say about them. In the present play, for instance, these two princes have seldom been noticed, and the few slight criticisms upon them seem to me very unsatisfactory. Henry Morley takes Morocco to represent "the love of money and what money can buy," while Arragon represents "the pride of rank." The latter statement is obviously true, but the former is absolutely without support in the text. Koenig thinks that "what Morocco calls love is nothing but a desire to possess Portia for her wealth and her fair reputation, — a purely superficial affection, not an honest love down deep in the heart"; and "Portia's assurance that he stood as fair as any other of her suitors conveys to us, who know what her feelings towards those others are, a keen satire, which becomes extremely comic when Morocco thanks her for it." Now, to me nothing can be clearer than that Morocco has an honest love for Portia, while Arragon has not. We might expect that, in a pair of scenes necessarily so much alike as these in which the two princes try their luck with the caskets, the dramatist would endeavour to give variety in this way, which is the only one natural or possible; and we might expect, also, that he would make Portia recognize the difference in the two suitors, and that this would inevitably affect her treatment of them. This is precisely what we find on a careful reading of the scenes. Morocco is permitted to appear twice, — a significant fact in itself. In the first scene he apparently meets Portia for the first time, and, although he has come to Belmont as a mere adventurer for the golden fleece, he falls in love with the lady at sight, and avows it at once. She cannot help pitying him, and tells him, with gentle courtesy, that she is not free to choose a husband, but that, if she were, he would stand as fair a chance as any suitor who has yet come to try the fortune of the caskets. He is the only one of these who has really loved her. Bassanio has *not* come, and she has no reason to expect him. There is no " satire " in what she says, and nothing " comic " in Morocco's reply. With the intuition of a lover, he detects the sympathetic touch in her words, and thanks her for it. There is a lover's delicacy in the expression of his gratitude : " *even for that* I thank you." It is not much in the way of encouragement, but, in his " poverty of grace," he thankfully takes what he can get, and only very timidly intimates his hope for more hereafter. He begs that he may go to his trial at once, though, blind Fortune being the arbiter, he may miss the prize " and die with grieving." Portia tells him that he must take his chance, reminding him that if he chooses wrong he can court no other lady. " Nor will not ! " is the prompt and expressive response. If he fails, he will be the " cursed'st among men," with no heart for further wooing. When he stands before the caskets, he hastily rejects the lead, because it " threatens," but tarries long in consideration of the silver, which promises " as much as he deserves." His own desert, he thinks, " may not extend so far as to the lady." There spoke the true lover; but, like a true lover, he takes heart again, and dares to hope he may deserve her. His birth and breeding and fortune equal hers, " but *more than these*," he adds, " *in love* I do deserve,"

— and that is no utterance of "a purely superficial affection," as the German critic calls it. But before making his choice he will look at the "saying graved in gold." "What many men desire! Why, that's the lady!" And to the end of the speech the one theme is "the lady." Alas! it is his exalted idea of her that leads to the fatal decision. It were damnation to imagine her heavenly picture shut up in the base lead; nor can she, who is ten times undervalued to tried gold, be immured in the inferior silver. Nothing worse than gold can be the setting of so rich a gem; the "angel" (whereon he puns in pretty loverlike fashion) can repose only in a golden bed. But it is a carrion skull, not fair Portia's counterfeit, that he finds in the deluding gold. He must depart, but he has too grieved a heart to take a tedious leave. "A gentle riddance," is the kindly comment of the lady when he is gone.

Enter now the Prince of Arragon, who loves himself better than he loves the lady, — whose fortune, nevertheless, he fain would have. He goes to the trial in business-like fashion, first making sure that the conditions are clearly understood. The gold is not for him, because he scorns to choose what many men desire; but the silver appeals to his self-sufficiency. He will "assume desert," and demands the key of the casket. "Too long a pause for that which you find there," Portia cannot help saying, disgusted as she is with the arrogant fool. Capell made this speech an *aside*, because, if addressed to Arragon, it has "the sound of twitting him," which he thinks is not quite in character. It may possibly be an *aside*, but it is quite in keeping with what she says to him afterwards. He considers himself ill-treated. When he finds the portrait of the blinking idiot, he says: —

> "How much unlike art thou to Portia!
> How much unlike my hopes and *my deservings!*
> 'Who chooseth me shall have as much as he deserves.'
> Did *I* deserve no more than a fool's head?
> Is that my prize? Are *my deserts* no greater?"

Still " my deserts," as throughout his soliloquy before the caskets, and not a word about "the lady," who was the entire burden of Morocco's musings. What could be more cutting than Portia's quiet reply? —

> " To offend and judge are distinct offices,
> And of opposed natures."

His offence is in having made a fool of himself; and, being a fool, he cannot see himself as others see him. Portia intimates pretty plainly what *her* judgment would be; and, in his impotent wrath at the issue of his mercenary wooing, he unwittingly passes a similar sentence upon himself in his next speech : —

> " With one fool's head I came to woo,
> But I go away with two."

How much unlike the parting of the heart-stricken if not heart-broken Morocco ! "Thus hath the candle singed the moth ! " is Portia's contemptuous comment to Nerissa after the baffled fortune-hunter has gone.

GRATIANO AND NERISSA. — The loves of Gratiano and Nerissa are kept duly subordinate to those of Bassanio and Portia. Shakespeare's fine discrimination is apparent even in the minutest details of the delineation of the two couples. In the trial scene, for instance, the marked difference in speeches that at first sight seem almost identical may be noted : —

> " *Bassanio.* Antonio, I am married to a wife
> Which is as dear to me as life itself;
> But life itself, my wife, and all the world,
> Are not with me esteem'd above thy life.
> I would lose all, ay, sacrifice them all
> Here to this devil, to deliver you.
>   *Portia.* Your wife would give you little thanks for that,
> If she were by to hear you make the offer.
>   *Gratiano.* I have a wife, whom, I protest, I love;
> I would she were in heaven, so she could
> Entreat some power to change this currish Jew.

> *Nerissa.* 'Tis well you offer it behind her back;
> The wish would make else an unquiet house."

If this dialogue were shown to a person wholly unacquainted with the rest of the play, and he were asked which pair were the more refined in character, and probably the higher in the social scale, would he have any difficulty in answering the question?

Nerissa, as Hunter remarks (*New Illustrations of Shakespeare*, 1845) is "not a waiting-maid, in the modern sense of the term," but "a young lady," such persons being often found in that day "attending on ladies of superior distinction and fortune." She belongs to the same class as Lucetta in *The Two Gentlemen of Verona*, Ursula and Margaret in *Much Ado*, Maria in *Twelfth Night*, and Helena in *All's Well*.

Gratiano is a gentleman, like Salanio and Salarino, but not the equal of Bassanio in rank and social standing. He goes to Belmont with Bassanio as a companion or attendant, apparently holding for the time being somewhat the same position with reference to his friend as Nerissa does to Portia. Bassanio, as we see (ii. 2. 182, fol.), thinks it necessary to give him some serious counsel as to his behaviour while at Belmont.

I may add what Mrs. Jameson says of the pair: "Nerissa is a clever, confidential waiting-woman, who has caught a little of her lady's elegance and romance; she affects to be lively and sententious, falls in love, and makes her favour conditional on the fortune of the caskets, and in short, mimics her mistress with good emphasis and discretion. Nerissa and the gay, talkative Gratiano are as well matched as the incomparable Portia and her magnificent and captivating lover."

JESSICA. — The pretty daughter of the Jew is charming in her way, and we do not wonder that Lorenzo, who is a romantic young fellow, falls in love with her; but she has little filial feeling. Her cool robbery of her father — it *is* cool, as we see from her jesting about it (ii. 6. 49) while committing it — proves that she is lacking in moral sense no less than in natural affection. But what has Shylock done to make the girl love him or to cultivate her moral perceptions? What has she seen in him but miserly greed, unfeeling exaction, virtual robbery of the unfortunate; and in his treatment of his family a niggardly parsimony that proved his love of gold to be paramount to his affection for his own flesh and blood? Brought up under such influences and with such surroundings, is it strange that she feels no scruple in plundering the father who has cheated her young life out of its dues of paternal love, education, and kindness — even out of its fair share of the good things of a merely material sort to which the child of a rich man is entitled? As his only heir she feels that she may help herself to what honestly belongs to her, and take by stealth the dowry she can secure in no other way. If we cannot quite justify her conduct, we are, nevertheless, compelled to recommend her to mercy. This, we may be sure, was the poet's unspoken verdict in the case.

Some critics have been severe upon her for eloping with Lorenzo, and "leaving her poor old father" to his solitary existence; for it is evident that Leah died long ago. But, as Jessica says, "Our house is hell," where even the foolery of that merry devil, Launcelot, will be seriously missed when he goes to a new master. And Shylock is not the aged man he is often represented on the stage. It is doubtful whether we should regard him as more than fifty. According to Hazlitt, Kean did not make him "the decrepit old man, bent with age," that had formerly been the theatrical Jew. He was, we may believe, still strong in body as in mind, and well able to take care of himself after his daughter has gone. In his reproaches of her he says nothing of his dependence upon her filial attentions and services.

The Law in the Trial Scene

According to one of the early traditions concerning Shakespeare, he was an attorney's clerk for a time before he left Stratford for

London; and the many references, literal and figurative, in his works to technicalities of the law, especially such as are not likely to become known to non-professional people, have led Lord Campbell and other specialists to believe that he must have studied law somewhat thoroughly; but Judge Allen, of the Supreme Judicial Court of Massachusetts, in his recent *Notes on the Bacon-Shakespeare Question* (1900), has shown that such legal allusions are equally common in other dramatists of the time, and that Shakespeare, instead of being uniformly accurate in these matters, as Lord Campbell and others have assumed, is often guilty of mistakes which a lawyer or student of law would never make. This may be regarded as the final word on the question of the supposed legal attainments of the dramatist.

Much has been written on the law in the present play, some taking the ground that it favours the theory of Lord Campbell, while others say it proves that the play could not have been written by one acquainted with law. For an interesting summary of the discussion, see Furness's "New Variorum" edition of the play, pp. 403–420, besides scattered notes on the subject elsewhere in the volume. Only one or two points can be referred to here.

The mention of a "single bond" in i. 3. 141 has been cited in support of both sides of the controversy. Lord Campbell says: "This bond to Shylock is prepared and talked about according to all the forms observed in an English attorney's office. The distinction between a 'single bond' and a 'bond with a condition' is clearly referred to." But Shylock's bond is obviously a bond with a condition, and therefore is not "single" in the legal sense. For myself, I believe (see note on the passage) that it means "individual bond, or one without sureties." The term is used in its popular sense, not in a technical one. It would perhaps be refining overmuch to suppose that Shylock craftily employs it in the latter sense because he wants to make the "condition" appear like none at all, — merely the "merry sport" he calls it; as if he had said, "Give me your bond without any condition, — at least none worthy of the name or to be legally enforced, — though for the joke of the thing we will say that I am to have a pound of your flesh if you fail to pay up at the appointed time." I have sometimes been inclined to explain the passage in that way. Observe that, a moment later, Shylock refers to the " condition " as only a nominal one :

> " If he should break his day, what should I gain
> By the exaction of the forfeiture ? "

He implies that he has no intention of exacting it, so the bond is virtually ",single," or to be treated as such.

As to the obviously " bad law " in the trial scene, which some critics ascribe to Shakespeare's ignorance of law, we must bear in mind that he took it from the familiar story on which the play was partly founded, and that it was too effective on the stage to be omitted. But it is a significant fact — to me, at least, for I believe that no commentator or critic has referred to it — that the dramatist, after using this " bad law " from the old tale, makes Portia go on to say :

> " Tarry, Jew;
> The law hath yet another hold on you," —

namely, on account of his having sought the life of Antonio. Note at what length this is dwelt upon, and how much stress Portia lays upon it. Note also that this is not in the various forms of the old story, but is Shakespeare's own addition thereto. I have no doubt that he added it solely because he knew that the original " law " was " bad," and was not willing to rest the case upon it, as an inferior dramatist might not improbably have done. He kept the " bad law " for stage effect, but added the " good law " to satisfy his conscience or his sense of justice.

The Time–Analysis of the Play

In his paper " On the Times or Durations of the Action of Shakspere's Plays " (*Transactions of New Shakspere Society,*

1877–1879), Mr. P. A. Daniel sums up the "time-analysis" thus: —

"Time: eight days represented on the stage; with intervals. Total time: a period of rather more than three months.

Day 1. Act I.
        Interval — say a week.[1]
" 2. Act II. sc. i.–vii.
        Interval — one day.[2]
" 3. Act II. sc. viii. and ix.
        Interval — bringing the time to within a fortnight of the maturity of the bond.
" 4. Act III. sc. i.
        Interval — rather more than a fortnight.[3]
" 5. Act III. sc. ii.–iv.
" 6. Act III. sc. v., Act IV.
" 7 and 8. Act V."[4]

List of Characters in the Play

In this list the numbers in parentheses indicate the lines the characters have in each scene.

[1] In ii. 2, we find Launcelot lamenting his hard life in Shylock's service; and later he becomes the servant of Bassanio. Meanwhile Bassanio has engaged his ship, and is waiting for a fair wind; and Lorenzo has been courting Jessica. Note also what Jessica says in iii. 2. 279 fol. All this supposes a lapse of time — say a week — since the signing of the bond.   [2] For Bassanio's journey to Belmont, etc.

[3] In iii. 1, Shylock says to Tubal: "Go, Tubal, fee me an officer; bespeak him a *fortnight* before." This indicates an interval, between this and the preceding scenes, of sufficient length to bring the three-months bond to within a fortnight of its maturity.

[4] After the trial Bassanio and Antonio propose to fly towards Belmont early next morning. Portia and Nerissa start for home that night, and arrive on the next night (Day 7) before their husbands. Act V. begins at a late hour that night, and ends two hours before day (Day 8).

Duke of Venice: iv. 1 (57). Whole number, 57.

Prince of Morocco: ii. 1 (32), 7 (71). Whole number, 103.

Prince of Arragon: ii. 9 (66). Whole number, 66.

Antonio: i. 1 (46), 3 (39); ii. 6 (6); iii. 3 (19); iv. 1 (66); v. 1 (12). Whole number, 188.

Bassanio: i. 1 (51), 3 (16); ii. 2 (38); iii. 2 (144); iv. 1 (50); v. 1 (42). Whole number, 341.

Salanio: i. 1 (11); ii. 4 (3), 8 (21); iii. 1 (24). Whole number, 59.

Salarino: i. 1 (41); ii. 4 (3), 6 (5), 8 (34); iii. 1 (22), 3 (4). Whole number, 109.

Gratiano: i. 1 (34); ii. 2 (18), 4 (3), 6 (20); iii. 2 (31); iv. 1 (33), 2 (5); v. 1 (34). Whole number, 178.

Lorenzo: i. 1 (6); ii. 4 (27), 6 (21); iii. 2 (5), 4 (12), 5 (34); v. 1 (76). Whole number, 181.

Shylock: i. 3 (134); ii. 5 (39); iii. 1 (72), 3 (16); iv. 1 (103). Whole number, 364.

Tubal: iii. 1 (16). Whole number, 16.

Launcelot: ii. 2 (120), 3 (5), 4 (6), 5 (15); iii. 5 (35); v. 1 (7). Whole number, 188.

Old Gobbo: ii. 2 (41). Whole number, 41.

Salerio: iii. 2 (20); iv. 1 (4). Whole number, 24.

Leonardo: ii. 2 (2). Whole number, 2.

Balthazar: iii. 4 (1). Whole number, 1.

Stephano: v. 1 (8). Whole number, 8.

Servant: i. 2 (5); ii. 9 (11); iii. 1 (2). Whole number, 18.

Musician: iii. 2 (9). Whole number, 9.

Portia: i. 2 (96); ii. 1 (17), 7 (9), 9 (20); iii. 2 (118), 4 (71); iv. 1 (138), 2 (12); v. 1 (108). Whole number, 589.

Nerissa: i. 2 (46); ii. 9 (6); iii. 2 (5), 4 (2); iv. 1 (22), 2 (4); v. 1 (25). Whole number, 110.

Jessica: ii. 3 (16), 5 (4), 6 (18); iii. 2 (7), 4 (1), 5 (29); v. 1 (14). Whole number, 89.

"All": iii. 2 (1). Whole number, 1.

In the above enumeration, parts of lines are counted as whole lines, making the total in the play greater than it is. The actual number of lines in each scene (Globe edition numbering) is as follows: i. 1 (186), 2 (147), 3 (183); ii. 1 (46), 2 (215), 3 (21), 4 (40), 5 (57), 6 (68), 7 (79), 8 (53), 9 (101); iii. 1 (136), 2 (330), 3 (36), 4 (84), 5 (96); iv. 1 (458), 2 (19); v. 1 (307). Whole number in the play, 2662.

INDEX OF WORDS AND PHRASES EXPLAINED

233

An Introduction to the

Study of American Literature

By BRANDER MATTHEWS
Professor of Literature in Columbia University

Cloth, 12mo, 256 pages . . . . Price $1.00

A text-book of literature on an original plan, and conforming with the best methods of teaching.

Admirably designed to guide, to supplement, and to stimulate the student's reading of American authors.

Illustrated with a fine collection of facsimile manuscripts, portraits of authors, and views of their homes and birthplaces.

Bright, clear, and fascinating, it is itself a literary work of high rank.

The book consists mostly of delightfully readable and yet comprehensive little biographies of the fifteen greatest and most representative American writers. Each of the sketches contains a critical estimate of the author and his works, which is the more valuable coming, as it does, from one who is himself a master. The work is rounded out by four general chapters which take up other prominent authors and discuss the history and conditions of our literature as a whole. The book also contains a complete chronology of the best American literature from the beginning down to the present period.

Each of the fifteen biographical sketches is illustrated by a fine portrait of its subject and views of his birthplace or residence and in some cases of both. They are also accompanied by each author's facsimile manuscript covering one or two pages. The book contains excellent portraits of many other authors famous in American literature.

Copies sent, prepaid, on receipt of the price.

American Book Company

NEW YORK • **CINCINNATI** • **CHICAGO**
(S. 01)

A HISTORY OF
ENGLISH LITERATURE

BY

REUBEN POST HALLECK, M.A. (Yale)

Price, $1.25

HALLECK'S History of English Literature is a concise and interesting text-book of the history and development of English literature from the earliest times to the present. While the work is sufficiently simple to be readily comprehended by high school students, the treatment is not only philosophic, but also stimulating and suggestive, and will naturally lead to original thinking.

The book is a history of literature and not a mere collection of biographical sketches. Only enough of the facts of an author's life are given to make students interested in him as a personality, and to show how his environment affected his work. The author's productions, their relation to the age, and the reasons why they hold a position in literature, receive treatment commensurate with their importance.

At the end of each chapter a carefully prepared list of books is given to direct the student in studying the original works of the authors treated. He is told not only what to read, but also where to find it at the least cost.

AMERICAN BOOK COMPANY

NEW YORK   CINCINNATI   CHICAGO

(S. 90)